Harvey,
May you (
see all the [illegible]
[illegible] Michigan.
2009

Up North in Michigan

Up North in Michigan

A PORTRAIT OF PLACE IN FOUR SEASONS

JERRY DENNIS

University of Michigan Press • *Ann Arbor*

For Midori

Contents

Introduction

When you talk too much about a place there can be consequences. Twice in recent years I've been approached by people I didn't know, one from Texas, the other from Indiana, who confided shyly and with kind intentions that they had uprooted their families and moved to northern Michigan because I had written so glowingly about it in my books. I was shocked to hear it. That such a momentous life change could be inspired by books is surprising enough in this age when they barely make a blip on the cultural Richter scale. But to be the cause of such a change is astonishing. Also, of course, flattering. And, above all, confusing. What a responsibility! My friends are not amused. They stare into their beer mugs and mutter that the place is too crowded already. Damn it, Dennis, I can't hardly get a seat in a restaurant. Will you please just shut up?

I've tried, I really have. But apparently I can't help myself.

For as long as I can remember I've been fascinated with physical landscapes and with the lakes, rivers, forests, deserts, prairies, towns, and cities within them. I've wondered what makes a place unique, what defines it, what it is that allows us to perceive a "sense" of it and render a version of it with images and words. It's been my not very secret wish to study every place on earth, but of course one lifetime isn't enough for such a task, so I've taken to heart the words of Eudora Welty: "One place understood helps us understand all places better."

The place I understand best, and the one where I've lived all but a few of my years, is northern Michigan. It's where I grew up, where I met the love of my life, where we raised our family. I've never lost interest in it. And the funny thing is, after exploring it in every season,

1

in every kind of weather, on foot, on bicycle, in canoes, cars, and from airplanes, I've barely scratched the surface.

Northern Michigan is two places: the northern third of the Lower Peninsula—which is what many of us mean when we say "northern Michigan"—and the Upper Peninsula or the "U.P." A general term for both places is simply "up north." Thus the title of this book.

Lately I've been asking my friends what up north means to them. One said it's the place where I-75 climbs from the agricultural flatlands of the Saginaw Valley into the rolling wooded hills around West Branch, where she can "relax and breathe again." Another said he thinks of the place in sensory terms: the scent of pines, the taste of onshore breezes from the Great Lakes, the gurgling of trout steams. For another it means crossing the Mackinac Bridge and going back in time to a post-World-War-Two America of deer camp, old hotels and bars, and supper clubs where you can still find a seven-dollar T-bone steak. Yet another said that all the things he likes best about up north— hunting, fishing, and hanging out in "good ol' dive bars where you can shoot the shit with the locals"—get better the farther north he goes.

It's a place, like all places, in change. Much of the northern Michigan of my childhood has been bulldozed, subdivided, and built upon. Climate change is warming the water of the Great Lakes at an alarming rate—Lake Superior is now the fastest-warming large body of freshwater on the planet—creating increasingly frequent and severe storm events, altering aquatic and shoreline ecosystems, and contributing to further invasions by non-native plants and animals.

But the essence of the place hasn't changed. Millions of acres of state and national forests and other public lands remain intact, providing crucial habitat for wildlife and recreation for humans. Most of the lakes and rivers are still healthy and clean. Many small towns and much of the rural landscape have changed little in half a century. Why the place has not been devoured by the machinery of progress is not a mystery: countless dedicated people—and dozens of land conservancies, conservation organizations, and other advocacy groups—have worked very hard over the years to protect it. Their work will be appreciated for generations.

How much we see in the world depends, of course, on how willing we are to look. To get to know a place we can study its geology, botany, climatology, human history—but that's just a start. A more profound knowledge enters through our feet and fingertips, and makes its way into our bones as surely as sand makes its way into wood grain. It takes time. Years. Decades. Maybe a lifetime.

I can't imagine a more rewarding way to live.

Spring

Loon Song

They say spring advances fifteen miles a day, about the pace of a lei-surely walk, which explains how I could experience three of them last year.

The first was in March, in northern Ohio, along the shore of Lake Erie's Maumee Bay, where I stayed much of the month in a cabin near the bay. Mornings I rose early to look for songbirds in the woods and to watch hawks and vultures riding the thermals northward. I counted more than two hundred broad-wings one day, which I thought was spectacular, but a local birder said they sometimes numbered in the thousands, even tens of thousands—so many kettles speckled with wheeling hawks that they looked like spiral galaxies drifting through the universe. In the marshes and woodlots were other early migrants, such as red-winged blackbirds, ruby-crowned kinglets, yellow-rumped warblers, and a brown thrasher that perched on the topmost branch of a tree beside my cabin every morning and performed a dazzling reper-toire of "look-at-me, I'm-a-pretty-bird" arias.

Many of those same birds were 300 miles north when I returned home to northern Michigan in April. During my absence the snow had melted from our yard, and in the woods the forsythia and trillium were about to blossom. In the interval between maple sap running and the buds on the trees swelling to the size of mouse ears, spring had slipped in. Suddenly mayflies were hatching in the rivers, morels were popping beneath the aspens, and a dozen kinds of warblers were flitting in the high branches.

Then it was May and time for the third spring, so I drove 150 miles north, crossed the Mackinac Bridge and the Upper Peninsula to Sault Ste. Marie, Ontario, then turned northwest on Highway 17, the Trans-Canada Highway. You don't have to go far in that direction to find wild country. The highway follows the most rugged and least developed shoreline of Lake Superior—of any of the Great Lakes—where not many people live and the greatest traffic hazard is moose walking on the road at night. To the north are a couple provincial roads and a railroad line, but otherwise there's nothing but hundreds of miles of boreal forest, wild rivers, and unnamed lakes all the way to James Bay.

Past Batchawana I turned off the highway and followed a gravel road until it ended at a friend's cabin on the shore of Superior. I had the key but needed to shovel through a three-foot drift of crusty snow before I could open the door. The winter had been harsh in Ontario, with greater than average snowfall, and so cold that much of Lake Superior had frozen over, a rare occurrence in the 21st century. Now the ice was gone from the lake—it was nothing but blue water all the way to the horizon—though a few remnants of icebergs were stranded on the beach. I looked up and saw a dozen broad-winged hawks circling overhead, regrouping, I supposed, after crossing the lake from Michigan's Whitefish Point. Maybe they were the same birds that had passed over Ohio in March.

Spring is the most complicated season. It approaches incrementally, pulling its clanging train of machinery, and a few weeks in we realize that the name we've given it is wrong. It doesn't spring, it sidles, two steps forward and one back, and then it halts altogether, like a child in a sulk, and you have to wait through another week of cold and snow before it eases forward again. A single name isn't enough for this reluctant, dawdling season. It could have a dozen, at least. Crocus in the Snow. Dripping Eaves. Leaf-buds Open. Oriole's Return.

The first night at the cabin on Lake Superior I stood on the stone-shingled beach and looked up at the stars. The Milky Way was a brilliant wide brushstroke from horizon to horizon, the stars as bright as those I remember from childhood. Out on the water their reflections filled the bowl of this lake that is as big as some nations. Everything above and before me was open, exposed, vast. When I was a child, growing up in the woodlands, so much open space was sometimes disorienting, even oppressive. But now it felt liberating.

In the morning I woke to the "Old Sam Peabody, Peabody, Peabody" call of a white-throated sparrow outside my window. I stepped from the cabin into a warm south wind carrying a patchwork of complex scents. There was a gust of warmth smelling of beach, then a refrigerated puff laden with the big-water scent of the lake, then micro-gusts carrying hints of pine and sweet-fern. At first I couldn't see the sparrow, then spotted it on a branch behind the cabin, backlit against the sky, just as it tipped back its head and cut loose again with its song. Another familiar call sounded high overhead and I looked up to see a loon hurtling past, bound for the far north of Canada. Then another, and another, each trailing a string of ululating warbles.

It was the clarion announcement, the anthem of the wild north, a song that stirs longing in those of us who cherish our few remaining unspoiled places. It's the music of mist-shrouded lakes surrounded by spruce forest, a boreal timelessness winding down in this age of accelerating change. Coming from the sky above Superior it was the sound of wildness in transit, winging north with the lengthening days of this season of hope.

Spring Arrives

Spring! Is it any wonder we grow impatient for it in March, when the calendar promises the season is changing but the weather has other ideas? We step outside hoping to hear the bassoon rumble of frogs in the neighbor's pond—and instead are struck by a cold wind from the north and a rattle of sleet.

I remember a spring many years ago that arrived even more slowly than most. It was 1979, the year that thirty-two feet of snow fell on the Keweenaw Peninsula in Michigan's Upper Peninsula and a succession of blizzards swept across the U.S. and Canada, shutting down cities from the Rockies to the East Coast. I was a student that year at Northern Michigan University in Marquette, living in the U.P. for the first time and already in love with it. During one particularly severe storm I watched astonished as the temperature—actual, not wind-chill—plummeted to 20 below zero Fahrenheit, then 30 below, then 50 below. Lake Superior froze from shore to shore that winter, as it had only a few times in half a century, and snowbanks rose so high above the streets in Marquette that pedestrians walking the goat trails on top could have easily reached up and touched the telephone wires.

By April everyone I knew was ready for spring, but the wait was becoming discouraging. I walked a mile to the campus every day and noticed with interest that as April progressed the buds on the trees and shrubs remained as tight as fists. The snow settled to a few feet of dirty crust, but would melt no further. The days stayed a cheerless 25 degrees, and the nights fell to the teens. The sky remained cloud-covered and dark.

The last Saturday of the month, the opening day of trout season, I set out in an act of defiance to fish a small river I had discovered the previous summer. I'd been thinking all winter about a stretch of that river flowing through a secret valley of cedars surrounded by abandoned farmlands, but the two-track road leading to it was blocked with snow so I had no choice but to hike over the ice-crusted snow carrying my waders and unstrung fly rod. When I reached the river it was flowing high, dark, and dangerous, so I didn't bother putting my waders on. Instead I walked the bank, pretending to look for trout, but watching, in truth, for spring.

It arrived in the afternoon, when the clouds opened just as an ice dam upstream burst, sending a knee-high wave of ice and slush surging past where I stood on the bank. The river rose two feet and changed to the color of freshly stomped mud puddles. The air temperature jumped 5 or 10 degrees, the sun turned the cedars from gray to green, and birds began singing. Hope surged through me and I hurried to string up my fly rod, attach a bead-head nymph, and make a few casts into the murky water. No trout showed themselves, but I didn't expect them to. Almost immediately the sun disappeared behind the clouds, the birds went silent, and my ears burned with cold again. But no matter—spring had arrived, with fanfare.

Water, Water

We've never suffered much cabin fever in my family, thanks to ice fishing and snowshoeing, a well-stocked home library, and a robust game of living-room hockey my sons and I played when they were young, using a tennis ball for a puck and bookcases for goals. But winter is long in northern Michigan, and by March we're always eager for spring. It comes in slow-moving stages: a patch of yellow grass in the yard and a warmish south wind carrying those aromas of new growth and freshly turned soil that people through the ages have always associated with promise. But for us the promise isn't delivered until we can walk down the road to East Bay and see bright stones in the water and waves breaking on the sand. The first day of real spring always sends us straight to the nearest water.

We're not alone in this. Countless people—probably the majority of us—are drawn to lakes, rivers, ponds, and oceans when we need to refresh or recreate. We fish, paddle, sail, ski, swim, snorkel, dive, or just hang out on the beach. It seems to be a universal compulsion. Almost without knowing it, we're attracted to water.

Its appeal is so strong that we invest it with special powers and make token sacrifices to it, throwing coins in fountains just as our ancestors did to propitiate gods they believed had the power to withhold rain or send it in floods. Water has always awakened both our sense of wonder and our fears, which is surely why it has inspired more lyrical expression from artists, poets, and composers than any other aspect of the natural world. We're mesmerized by water's flow and fall, by the voices we hear in it and the colors we see in it, by the elegant shapes of its waves, raindrops, and snowflakes. We're drawn to waterfalls and crashing surf because they're powerful enough to pull us out of our ordinary selves. There's something exhilarating about that—maybe because it reawakens us to things that captivated us as children.

When I was a kid my brother and I had a spring ritual that seems reckless to me now but was irresistible to us then. As the ice began to break up on Long Lake it would melt first around the edges, opening a band of water that ringed the shore as far as we could see. As soon as it was wide enough to accommodate a boat, Rick and I would turn over the aluminum rowboat that had been stored all winter on shore and slide it into the water. We would step inside, fit the oars in the locks, and push off.

The water was so clear that the stones on the bottom were revealed in crisp detail. Among them rested the skeletons of drowned maple leaves, their veins as delicate as the bones of mice. I knew waves would wash them away when the lake was fully open, but for now they were preserved as if under glass.

Already the ice covering most of the lake had decayed and turned very dark and irregular. We could see the scars of holes that had been left weeks ago by ice fishermen, some of them marked with a twig or evergreen swag to keep the unwary from stepping in them. Every year one or two shanties had been abandoned on the ice and were now slowly sinking into the lake.

Rick and I knew enough to stay off the ice when it reached this stage of decay, but we discovered that when we rammed the ice with the boat or struck it with the oars it would crumble into crystalline, hexagonal shards, creating more open water. Better yet, if the wind was blowing cracks would open large enough for us to enter in our boat. We pushed rafts of slush out of the way, then used our oars as push-poles to make our way along the jagged leads until we passed the drop-off where the water became so deep it was black.

If the leads were big enough we would go to Ann's Island, where we beached the boat and searched for any of Ann's rabbits that might have survived the winter. Later, when the ice was gone, our mother would row us to the island with bags of leftover lettuce and other vegetables to feed the rabbits. Often they were so hungry they would be lined up watching from the shore as we approached. Twenty years later Mom would lead her grandchildren on those same relief missions.

Sometimes while Rick and I were on the island the wind would close the leads and we would be stranded for a few hours. It was a delicious sort of emergency. What if nobody knew where we were? What if we were forced to build a campfire and spend the night? It never came to that but the possibility thrilled us, for of course we were on the lake not just to celebrate spring but to practice our independence.

It's not unusual in northern Michigan to step outside and in a single glance see snow, clouds, and dripping eaves—water in its solid, gaseous, and liquid forms. That it can exist in all three states simultaneously is just one remarkable quality of this most remarkable of substances. If, by midwinter, water's novelty has worn off, spring brings it back in a rush.

After a winter of sensory deprivation, getting outside reminds us that our veins flow with the same molecules as the lakes and rivers around us. Fishing, boating, swimming, and other activities allow us to know water in ways we might miss if all we did was watch it from a distance. The secret of the stuff, and perhaps the key to its fascination, is that it beckons us to come closer and become more immersed in the world.

The Color of Steelhead

One bright morning in April I walked the banks of a little river near my home, looking for steelhead. I was there to fish, but I was distracted. The scent of spring was in the air and trout lilies were poking above the floor of the woods where two weeks ago there was snow. In another week morels would appear. I would gather enough for a meal, cut them lengthwise, toss them in flour, fry them in butter, and serve them with grilled asparagus and—

Then I spotted her.

She was eight pounds, maybe ten, and so fresh from Lake Michigan that she gave off the silver-and-blue hues of the big lake itself. I almost didn't see her. A steelhead in a stream can disappear so completely it seems like a magician's trick. She was hovering in a narrow run of quick water no more than knee-deep, under a broken surface that made the light chaotic and camouflaged the bottom with swimming shadows. She was hardly more than a shadow herself, shimmering with a suggestion of life.

Brown trout are buttery, decorated with the colors of gravel, and appear to be made for running water. Brook trout are the deep green of a creek in the shadows of a cedar swamp. But anadromous rainbow trout—steelhead—are different. They appear to have been condensed from the cobalt depths of the sea where they spend most of their lives, miles from shore, charging through schools of shiners. When they enter a river they carry some of the ocean's deep mystery with them. And when you hook them they fight like ocean fish, bolting downstream, bound for hundred-foot depths, until, because a river is too small to hold them, they leap above it.

I cast a small orange fly into the river six feet upstream from her. It sank slowly and drifted with the current until it entered her line of sight. For a moment she seemed ready to attack, her pectoral fins extended, her shoulders tensing. I could have been twelve years old again, casting spawn bags into the Boardman River and hoping with all my heart that I would feel the tap-tap of a steelhead taking my bait. In those days I killed and carried home every steelhead I caught, but now I only want to bring them to hand, admire them for a moment, and release them back into the river.

I didn't move. Didn't breathe. Then, as the fly grew near, she started backing away. I've seen steelhead do this too many times to be surprised. She backed away until she entered the shallow water at the tail of the pool. Now I saw her clearly. Ten pounds, at least. So fresh from the lake that her sides were still chrome-colored, with not even a hint of the pink stripe that appears after a steelhead has been in the river for a few days. But she was not fooled by my fly. She flared in the current, turned, and with a powerful thrust was gone.

Soon she would spawn and return to the big lake. Her offspring would hatch, grow into smolts, and follow her to the lake. In a few years they would come back as adults to climb the river and try to fill the world with their progeny.

May they be successful. May they be prolific.

A Random Act

I went to the Betsie River to fish for steelhead, but the river was too crowded so I walked the bank and watched people instead. It was late in the spring run and the river was full of suckers—maybe a thousand suckers for every steelhead. Anglers standing on the banks would cast their lures and baits and wait in anticipation as their offerings bounced along the bottom. Now and then somebody would set the hook with a sudden yank of their rod and you would see a moment of excitement on their faces, then disappointment. Sucker. They knew immediately. A steelhead rips line from the reel and leaps wildly into the air. A friend who has caught hundreds of them says he always expects a steelhead to *roar* when it leaps. But a sucker doesn't have that much vitality. It is a plain, medium-sized fish that when hooked shakes its head slowly, as if half asleep, then allows itself to be towed to shore. Anglers reeled them in quickly and yanked the hooks from their mouths and some- times they released the fish but more often they tossed them onto the bank to die. When I was a kid I knew many people who fished for them intentionally, entire families filling buckets with suckers they would take home to can or smoke. But fewer people eat them now. Most consider them trash fish that apparently deserve to be thrown on the ground to die and rot.

As I watched, three boys approached the river at one of the bends. They were about twelve years old, that pivotal moment at the end of childhood. They cast their baits into the water and started catching suckers like everyone else. But unlike the other anglers, they enjoyed it. They would hook a sucker and yell in triumph, then fight it, land it, unhook it, and throw it onto the bank behind them. A dozen or more were already there, left by other anglers, lying among the discarded bottles and cans and snarls of monofilament line. Some of the fish were already dead. Others lay gasping, sometimes kicking their tails feebly. Now and then one managed to flip over, coating itself with dirt and leaves.

It was an ugliness I knew too well. I remembered my brother and I at that age experimenting with a glass jar, lighter fluid, and grasshoppers. It was shocking to discover how cruel we could be. Maybe killing helpless creatures was a way to feel more powerful—maybe an effort to take control over death itself—but for us the experiment failed. It made us sick at heart, and we never did anything like it again.

The boys at the Betsie River were treading similar ground but they seemed more hardened than my brother and I were, even at our most heartless. Their behavior confirmed my fear that as the world has grown more crowded we have become colder and more cruel.

Then I noticed that one of the boys was holding back from the others. When his friends turned away to cast their baits and could not see him, he put his foot against a sucker that was still alive on the ground and eased it into the river. He eased three or four others in the same way before rejoining his friends.

A compassionate soul, I thought, my heart lifting a little. But it's a rotten world—rotted straight to the core—when a child has to be afraid to show compassion.

An April Shower

We had the season's first thunderstorm the other day, and it couldn't have come at a better time. I was in my canoe, drifting with the current on the Boardman River below Garfield Road, when a belly rumble sounded over the hills to the west. It was a pristine day in late April—a little too pristine, if you asked me—and I was in the mood for some uproar. A rollicking good storm was just the ticket for launching us into summer.

I'm old enough now to be grateful for spring and young enough still to be a little giddy with it. Though I can get dewy-eyed about autumn—those crisp nights, the frost-spangled mornings, the brassy afternoons flavored with the certainty that winter is coming and can't be stopped—it's been impressed upon me lately that only the young can afford to romanticize decline. Once you get some gray in your hair, spring starts looking better every year.

I like it for all the usual reasons. Because it's the season of rebirth and renewal. Because it's optimistic. Because it fills us with some of the leap-in-the-air enthusiasms of youth and makes us want to grab a backpack and light out for the wilderness. A sort of caffeine energy surges through me, until I can't sit still another moment. Every year on the first warmish day in March I climb the south-facing hill behind our house and try to catch sight of spring. It's been marching north for weeks by then, making its fifteen miles a day, and taking its sweet time about it. It smells sweet, too. And clean. And temporary.

Rivers also are temporary. After all these years I still forget. This first trip of the season I was two bends below the bridge on Garfield Road before I realized that it was not the same river I had known in October. The Boardman is quick and spirited, a classic trout stream: spring-fed, clear, its riffles sun-drenched and its pools shaded by the lush leaning cedars we call "sweepers." I've known this river intimately for most of my life, yet it is always both familiar and strange, which is one reason I keep coming back. As many explorers of the near-at-hand have observed, if you can discover the new in the familiar, there's no reason to leave home. The trick, of course, is finding the new.

On a sweeping gravel bend where I have fished many times for trout, a large hemlock had fallen into the river, its dangling roots still gripping stones and its black trunk buried deep in the flow of the river. The current, diverted by this sudden obstruction, had gone to work dredging a new channel through the gravel, creating a waist-deep running pool where the water had previously been only ankle deep. At the next bend downstream an entire maple tree uprooted during a spring or winter freshet had run aground. It rested parallel to the current, narrowing the river by half, and had collected other pieces of driftwood that will provide shelter and sustenance for generations of trout and other river dwellers. Every year it's like discovering a new river.

In one of the last undeveloped stretches between Garfield and River Road, someone had finally broken ground for a house. Near the building site is an artesian well that spouts a constant fountain of sweet cold water ten feet into the air, as if from an opened hydrant, where for five decades I have refreshed myself every time I fished this section of the river. It's a nice piece of property. Very nice. I'd always secretly planned to own it myself someday. Now I have to brace myself for the no-trespassing signs that are sure to come.

After the sensory deprivations of winter, spring can overwhelm us with its bounty. Drifting down the river that day I saw wonders: Mayflies in the final few minutes of their lives riding the current with their wings upright and canted like tiny sloops. Small trout breaking the surface to feed on the mayflies, their subtle bulges and rings— "rise-forms" in angling jargon—erased in a moment by the current. On the banks were coiled green fiddleheads and trilliums about to bloom and vibernum sprouting their mauve mouse-ears. With the breeze came mixed odors of fertility and decay and the lush aroma of approaching rain. Beyond the hills, but much closer now, came another rumble of thunder.

I paddled into slack water and took shelter beneath a cedar. A few raindrops fell. Then a few more. A rushing sound came through the woods, and suddenly raindrops as heavy as nickels plummeted from the sky and struck the river with percussive notes, raising a multitude of spouts an inch high. The cedar above me became saturated and began to drip. The air grew rich with fragrance.

Then, as abruptly as the storm had arrived, it passed. I pushed into the current, dug deep with my paddle, and pulled the river toward me. The canoe jumped as if it had been spurred. The sun came out and lit the riffles with spangles and warmed my wet clothes until they steamed. All around me, birds sang insanely. I wanted to stand in the canoe and shout. The birds, the river, the trees with their buds about to burst into leaf, even by god the gray-haired guy yodeling in his canoe—the whole world was growing younger by the moment.

Opening Days

We had big plans for opening weekend. Our friends Kevin and Sharon in California had invited us to stay in their log cabin in the jack pines on the upper Manistee River. They call it a "cabin," but they're being modest. Kevin invited us also to float the river in his wooden Au Sable riverboat. He'd made the same invitation the previous year as well, but the boat is so splendid and pristine that I was worried about scratching it and never took it out of the garage. When Kevin found out he told me to stop being such a wuss. The boat's a tool, he said, it needs to be used. He insisted that scratches and gouges are not only permitted, they're required.

We planned to float the river Saturday morning—Jim and I in the riverboat, Gail and Mary Ann in kayaks. The women like to fish sometimes, but this weekend they were mostly interested in migratory songbirds and would carry binoculars and field guides instead of fly rods. In the afternoon the four of us would explore the woods around the cabin and try to hunt up some morels for dinner.

The temperature had been near 70 much of the week and promised to bring a buffet of mayflies. But Friday the temperature took a nosedive. So did the barometer. The wind that had been out of the south all week veered to dead north and started blowing whitecaps down the river. The temperature dropped ten degrees, then another ten degrees. Dark clouds rushed by, low enough to get snagged in the trees. Then the rain began. And then the snow.

I've enjoyed many opening days in rain and snow and a few times they've been among the best fishing days of the year. But that Saturday morning the four of us stood before the big windows and watched the wet snow falling into the river and decided it was a fine day to stay inside. Jim built a fire in the fireplace and Gail, Mary Ann, and I threw together a breakfast. Then we plundered Kevin's and Sharon's bookshelves and stretched out on the couches to read. The rain that had turned to snow now turned to sleet. I read two Elmore Leonard novels back-to-back. We napped. We played Yahtzee. The sleet turned to snow again.

That night, after the others had gone to bed, I stayed up late reading, stretched out on the couch in front of the fireplace. There was a moment of convergence as I was reading Jim Harrison's and Ted Kooser's collaborative book of poetry, *Braided Creek*, when I read the lines, "A frosty morning/and one mosquito at rest on the lip/of the tub"— and at that very moment a mosquito landed on my arm.

Around midnight I put on my boots and coat and went outside and stood in the snow and looked up at the black sky. The wind had died and now only a few snowflakes were falling. I walked down the stairs to the river and stood on the dock. The water flowed black and was silent, I thought, until I shut up and listened. Shushing sounds. Whispers. I let myself sink into it until I knew the relief of pure sound, stripped of meaning. It asked nothing of me. No interpretation was necessary, or even possible. No analysis, no deconstruction, no comparison to the sounds of other things in the world. The river keeps murmuring, and, best of all, it doesn't give a damn if we're listening.

It takes little effort to make a weekend in a cabin successful. In fact, the less effort the better. The weather craps out, so what? Build a fire and whip up a heart-attack breakfast and, while eating it, discuss what to have for lunch. The opening of trout season calls for a bottle of wine with lunch, and afterward maybe a sip or two of the single-malt scotch a friend sent along as a gift.

We didn't have fresh morels for dinner, but we managed to get by.

Our weekend in the jack pines brings to mind another trout opener, one two decades earlier, on another river. And it, too, had little to do with fishing.

My old friend Nute Chapman, who raised a large, robust family in a house he called Poverty Peak, near the village of Onaway, made opening day more ritualistic than anyone I've ever known. Every year he and his wife, Jean, hosted a trout camp at their house for their eight adult sons and daughters and an expanding herd of grandchildren. Now and then a lucky friend was invited to attend. Opening morning Nute would get up long before daylight and prepare a breakfast that would knock a crew of lumberjacks to their knees. By the time the kids arrived the kitchen table and counters were crowded with platters heaped with pancakes and waffles. There were loaves of home-made bread cut into slices so thick they jammed the toaster, and jars of the strawberry, tomato, and blueberry jams that Nute and Jean put up every year. There were eggs, bacon, sausage, and ham. And Nute stood by, grinning, calling for everyone to plate up and dig in.

I was a guest in 1990, when Nute was nearing 80 and could no longer wade the rivers he loved in Pigeon River Country. It was hard on him to stay home while everyone else fished, but he didn't complain. Instead he threw his considerable energy into feeding his mob and sending them off with sack lunches and advice on where to fish. While helping him pour coffee into thermoses I nodded at a twenty-inch brook trout mounted on the wall of the kitchen and asked him when it was caught. I assumed it was a relic from the golden days, when every pond and creek in northern Michigan swarmed with fish and it was still possible to find a brook trout twenty inches long. Nute said, "My oldest son got it last year, in a river not far from here." The tone of his voice made it clear there was no point in asking which river.

After breakfast, Nute's son Clark and I loaded our gear in Clark's pickup, strapped his canoe in the bed, and headed for a stretch of river I had never fished. It was barely daylight when we got there.

During the drive Clark had seemed distracted. Now, as we unloaded the canoe, I asked why, and he hemmed and hawed a little and finally admitted that his wife had gone into labor at three o'clock that morning. She was still in labor when he left the hospital to have breakfast at his folks' house. She was probably still in labor.

I was mortified. "You need to get to the hospital now!" I said.

"She told me she wanted us to fish," he said. "Hey, opening day only comes once a year."

We launched the canoe, floated a mile or so downriver, and caught a few brook trout. Then we hoofed it back to the truck, loaded our gear, and Clark drove me to my motel and continued on to the hospital. I called him later that day and learned that his wife had given birth to a beautiful, healthy daughter.

I never saw Nute again. He died the following winter. But I can guess how much his new granddaughter meant to him. A baby girl, a future member of Trout Camp, born on the best day of the year.

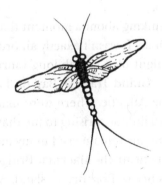

Night Watch on The Malabar

For a long time I had the wrong idea about adventure. I thought you had to risk your life. I thought you had to travel to distant places and put yourself in difficult situations. Now I know that ordinary moments can be adventures, too.

Lately I've been thinking about a moment that occurred one night in the Straits of Mackinac. It wasn't exactly an ordinary experience for me—it was the first night of a month-long journey to deliver a two-masted schooner from Grand Traverse Bay, on Lake Michigan, to Bar Harbor, Maine, on the Atlantic. There were many rowdy adventures ahead, which makes it a little surprising to me that after twenty years so many of the quiet moments remain vivid in my memory.

We had just passed beneath the Mackinac Bridge and were approaching the low, dark presence of Bois Blanc Island. Ahead was open Lake Huron, a black vastness stretching to the horizon. The night was cool, the wind still, and the Milky Way sprayed across the sky. It was the deep part of the night, when the stars are at their brightest.

I liked night watch. Often only the captain, Hajo Knuttle, and I were on deck, while the three other men on the crew slept below in their cabins. Many nights we stood together for hours at the helm and talked—or rather, Hajo talked and I listened, for he was a natural storyteller and had a mind that veered in unpredictable and fascinating directions. But at some point we always separated, one of us remaining at the helm and the other going forward to the bow to watch for other vessels.

Those hours were some of the most enjoyable of the journey. Being on the water was part of it, of course, but there were deeper satisfactions as well. One was simply being in motion, the boat cutting resolutely through the night. Probably it had a lot to do also with seeing new places, or old places from a new perspective. And it was exhilarating to be in the Straits of Mackinac, that crossroads of North American history and geography. For years I had been studying our mistreatment of the Great Lakes and of the native people whose lives and cultures have been entwined with them for millennia, and had grown disheartened. But here was a place that seemed, under the moonlight at least, to have changed little over the centuries.

Hours had gone by without much happening, but suddenly there came a moment of radiance. Nothing had changed, yet everything changed. It was *I* who had changed, I think. Suddenly I was seeing the world as it is, not through my usual lens. I saw, as if for the first time, that the lake in every direction around me was mirror smooth and bright with stars. And when I turned to look toward the stern I was startled to see a trail of moonlight stretching behind us to the Mackinac Bridge. The bridge arched in a spray of lights across the Straits, and above it was a gibbous moon casting its arrow of light onto the water.

A moment can swell to fill a bigger space. I wanted to stop the boat and let the moment fill me, too. I wanted time itself to stop. I needed the entire night—my entire life—to think about what I was seeing. Already I knew it would remain with me for as long as I lived.

The Overlooked Forest

A friend and I were walking one of our favorite trails in the trillium woods, where it follows a bluff above Lake Michigan and is worn so deep that two- and four-footed creatures must have been walking it for hundreds of years, when there came a sudden cracking noise and a huge beech tree split down the middle and crashed across the trail ahead of us. Bad luck if we'd set out half a minute earlier. Especially bad considering that it was a windless morning and the only apparent explanation was that the tree, after being stalwart for a century and a half, had surrendered in its war against gravity. It's the fate of all trees, but how often do we get to see it? Philosophers chuckle at the notion.

Suddenly we became more attentive to the trees, especially the ones we don't usually notice. Most of us recognize the A-listers—the maples, oaks, pines, and other glory-stealers—but our eyes slide across the dozens of smaller and less obvious species growing beneath them. Many are mid-story and under-story trees, less than forty feet high, that to the untutored eye just sort of melt into the background greenery. Timber cutters disdain them as "weed trees" because they have little commercial value, but maybe they're the real glories of the sylva, if only because they're so easy to miss that noticing them feels like a discovery.

In this part of the world they include mountain ash, Juneberry, box elder, pin cherry, crab apple, hawthorn. One of my favorites is striped maple, an elegant, almost dainty tree with delicately striped bark. It is found in northern hardwoods and mixed-wood forests from upper Michigan to Maine, Nova Scotia, and Newfoundland, and down the Appalachian Range as far south as Georgia. It's especially abundant in the Adirondacks of New York, where it's sometimes called Goosefoot Maple, for the shape of its leaf, or Moosewood, because moose eat its bark in winter. It has the lobed, oppositely attached leaves of the other maples but is a much smaller tree, usually less than fifteen to thirty feet in height and with a trunk that is rarely more than eight inches across. Not long ago I found a giant near Sleeping Bear Dunes, with a trunk ten inches in diameter and a height of at least thirty feet. It towered above its brethren like a sequoia. I've read that the Ojibwa valued the tree and made good use of it, stripping its inner bark and ingesting it as an emetic and fashioning arrows from its wood.

The aptly named ironwood, easily recognizable from its scalelike bark (one author refers to it as "scurfy"), was called hop hornbeam by early European settlers—hop for the clustered papery bags that enclose the fruit and nutlets; horn because the wood is so hard; beam because it makes enduring ones. Donald Peattie, in his wonderful *A Natural History of North American Trees*, explains that the "beam" in hornbeam is an Old English synonym for "tree," related to the German *Baum* familiar to us from "oh tannenbaum, oh tannenbaum." When I was an energetic young buck cutting cordwood on the weekends to earn extra money, I learned to leave ironwood untouched. Its knotty, twisted wood is loaded with BTUs and produces a splendid bed of coals, but cutting it into lengths is too much work. Sparks fly and the saw blade goes dull and all you get for the effort are a few chunks heavy as stone and impossible to split. You can see why early settlers preferred it for axe handles and pry bars.

It's a bountiful world beneath the big trees and, as always, the closer you get the more you see. The day the beech fell we left the trail and walked deeper into the untracked woods. At one point we paused beside a sassafras tree and picked a few of its leaves. It's easy to iden-tify sassafras from its irregular leaf lobes—two, one, or none per leaf, even on the same branch. The single-lobed leaves are mitten-shaped, endearing them to Michiganders. Native Americans gave the tree its name. It was they, too, who first learned to boil the bark and roots to produce the original root beer, a flavor you can taste in the leaf.

Then we glanced at the ground. Between our feet, sprouting from the leaf litter and surrounded by wild leeks and the bell-cluster blossoms of Dutchman's britches, was a cluster of morel mushrooms. A few yards away was another. And a pebble-toss away, another.

A day in the woods can be a bargain you make with the world. Take a little of the woods home, leave a little of yourself behind.

Drenched in Color

Now and then we need to escape. It seems to be a basic human impulse. In military terms retreat is disgraceful unless tactical. Ours are tactical. We retreat not from our responsibilities as parents, spouses, and citizens, but *into* our responsibilities as moral beings in need of replenishment. But why? What are we seeking? From what are we longing to escape? And why do we need it?

I was thinking these thoughts one spring afternoon while walking on a Lake Michigan beach. A mile down the shore was a cottage I had booked for a couple weeks of solitude after a period of too much work and too many human complications. Ahead was a curving shore of sandy beach and low dunes grown over with marram grass. The lake was calm, almost unnaturally so, and seemed to be colored a deeper blue than usual.

A grumble of thunder sounded behind me, and I turned and saw storm clouds approaching fast from the west. They were black and formidable and so low they nearly touched the bluffs above the shore. Deep inside were shuddering flashes of lightning. I stood, mesmerized, and watched a silver wall of rain rushing toward me. The drops that fell were so large I could see them kicking up spouts of sand on the beach.

In a moment the rain was on me, one of those instantaneous Niagara downpours that soaks you in seconds. I crouched to make myself a smaller target for lightning, but none showed anyway. The rain passed, and immediately the sky lightened and the sun pried the clouds apart. I turned and watched the back of the stormwall running away from me down the beach. The entire wall of cloud and rain was illuminated by the sun. It was strange to see those roiling black clouds lit so brightly, as if by floodlights during a dramatic moment on a stage, but overlit and overdesigned.

Suddenly—and nothing could have prepared me for this moment—everything around me was drenched in color. It was drenched from the rain, of course, but the greater drenching came from the light. A switch had been flipped and illumination was turned on with a roar. The receding black clouds, the sheets of rain angled beneath them, the pounded pewter surface of the lake, the sand on the beach, the bluffs and dunes—everything around me was suddenly so vivid, so clarified, that it was as if I were seeing the world for the first time.

Then I noticed the marram grass. It covered the backdunes in a sparse pelt, every blade leaning in the same direction and drenched in light so rich it seemed unnatural or otherworldly. The light had become a verb: it *greened* the marram, filled it with liquid light, made it luscious, redolent, ripe, natal, like spring's fresh growth but seven or eight shades brighter. It was the innocent green of the first spring morning, the green of all things vital and newborn. Years from now, when I think of my favorite escapes, I'll remember that greening.

From a Hilltop, Looking Back

In the woodlands northwest of Grayling a hill rises between two rivers. May is a good month to climb it and get some perspective. It was there that I found the place I'd been looking for: quintessential northern Michigan.

In the distance were the paper-torn silhouettes of glacial hills colored mauve and gray, marbled with bands of green. In the forests, I knew, were maple, beech, aspen, oak, hemlock, and pines. In the swamps and woods were bobcat, black bear, whitetail deer, ruffed grouse, turkey, coyote, elk. Not far east was a national forest containing a few hundred square miles of jack pine—that hardy, low-growing conifer that thrives in soil too poor to support much else—where virtually the entire world's population of Kirtland's warbler nest and raise their young.

Below me was the valley of the upper Manistee River. The river barely showed through the trees, but a winding ribbon of cedars marked its course.

Geographically this is not far from the highest point of the not-very-high Lower Peninsula, which is never more than about 1,700 feet above sea level. Ancient glaciers shaped this place, dredging and plowing and leaving behind hills of glacial debris that appear to roll across the land like earth waves. The topsoil is mostly sand and gravel in a water-permeable layer hundreds of feet deep in places. Surface water filters through it to replenish aquifers that eventually resurface as springs. The cold, clean water from those springs is the main reason the rivers and lakes are so hospitable to trout.

Here and there are farmlands gone wild, the remnants of home-steads that broke the hearts of farmers who were lured north by prom-ises of cheap land in the 19th and early 20th centuries. Most of those farmers long ago moved on when they were unable to scratch a living from the sandy soil. Only the hardiest and most resilient stayed on. Some of their descendants are still here, and still struggling to make a living.

I walked across the top of the hill a hundred yards to the east side and looked down on the valley of the upper Au Sable. The Au Sable and Manistee are at their nearest point here, flowing parallel for ten miles or so before diverging, the Manistee flowing south and west to Lake Michigan, the Au Sable south and east to Lake Huron.

This spot had been on my mind for years, since I learned that the Au Sable and Manistee formed one of the earliest cross-country canoe routes in Michigan. For centuries native people—and, later, European trappers, traders, and timber cruisers—paddled bark canoes up one river, portaged the height of land, and descended the other river, avoiding the long trip around the top of the mitten. Many of those early travelers probably made their way from one river to the other by way of Portage Creek and Lake Margrethe, with portages where necessary. Others might have chosen to portage over the very ridge where I stood.

Like so many places, this one has a shameful history of procure-ment. Shortly after the War of 1812, Lewis Cass, who would later become Michigan's first governor, persuaded the Chippewas to give up their claim to most of the northeast Lower Peninsula, from Saginaw Bay to Thunder Bay. It was there that some of the continent's larg-est stands of old-growth white pine grew. By 1842 most of the Indian lands had been claimed by the state—stolen, in fact—and tribes had been pushed to western territories beyond the Mississippi or isolated in small, local reservations.

In the 1830s and 1840s agents for the lumber barons paddled canoes up the Au Sable, Manistee, and virtually every other river until they reached the heart of the pine forests. The agents' reports described incredible bounty. They said you could see for hundreds of yards through those forests, beneath a canopy so dense no undergrowth could live there. The forests extended almost unbroken from the Saginaw Valley to the Straits of Mackinac—thousands of square miles of virgin pines and hardwoods, ripe for harvest.

It took a few decades for the loggers themselves to reach the interior. In the late 1800s a speculator named David Ward might have climbed this very hill searching for stands of pine, to which he promptly laid claim, eventually owning 70,000 acres on both sides of the Manistee. Ward built a mill on the river that grew into a small town that thrived for a while. The crumbling remains of concrete wing dams and building foundations are still there. On early plat maps the town was abbreviated as "D. Ward." Spoken aloud it became "Deward," which is how everyone refers to it today.

When the pines were gone, Ward turned to the hardwoods. Once they too were gone, leaving tens of thousands of acres of devastation, Ward and his crew moved on.

Today the traces of the early timber industry can still be seen. Weathered, lichen-covered stumps hollowed by time remain scattered through the woods and meadows, many of them charred from the fires that swept across the wasteland of slashings the loggers left behind. The stumps are so dense with resin that my father used to peel translucent curls away with his pocketknife and use them as fire starters. On cold days during deer season we would sometimes light a whole stump into a bonfire and gather around it to eat lunch. As we ate our sandwiches, my father, uncles, and cousins would stand in the billowing sweet smoke and tell stories.

The land is still crossed by the old two-track roads the loggers cleared to reach the timber. If you search diligently, it's even possible to find the remains of the old logging camps. My buddy Del Houghton and I discovered one once when we were boys. It was not far from Del's house, a few miles west of Long Lake, in a maple woodlot surrounded by fallow fields. First we stumbled across a heap of rusted kerosene lanterns, their glass globes broken or missing. As we kicked around in the weeds looking for treasure we glanced at a nearby maple three feet across at the trunk and found the rusted blade of a two-man crosscut saw emerging from its opposite sides. We concluded that loggers must have sawn partway through the tree, then for some reason walked away. The tree survived this indignity and grew around the saw. Del and I broke the two parts away and took them home to show our parents, who, I remember, were not greatly impressed.

Standing on the hill that day I saw the past and present entwined. Below me, on each side of the hill, I could pick out the logical routes a person might use to carry a canoe from one river to the other. Surely those same routes were evident hundreds or thousands of years ago.

It's good to climb a hill now and then and take stock. You can see the broad strokes, the overview, the bigger picture. You might find a fresh view of where you are in your life, how you got there, and maybe even where you're headed.

Looking down on the valley of the Manistee I caught a glimpse of silver through the cedars. Maybe it was the river, maybe a beaver pond that nobody knew about. Suddenly I lost interest in the long view and just wanted to catch some trout, so I hurried down the hill to the bottomlands, into the cedars and tag-alder thickets, and became happily lost in the short view.

Yellowthroats and Agates

In early May Gail and I often go to the Upper Peninsula to look for birds. We do a sort of Grand Tour, starting at Mackinac State Park, where the cedars are sometime teeming with warblers, drive west to the Seney Wildlife Refuge, then make our way north and east to Whitefish Point. Whitefish Point is renowned among birders as a "funnel" for migratory birds. It's not unusual in April and May to see hundreds of raptors of eight or ten species soaring in kettles as they wait for a favorable wind to help them across Whitefish Bay to Canada. Coastal ponds and wetlands and Whitefish Bay itself are often full of ducks and geese, as well as occasional yellowlegs, bitterns, rails, and other shy water birds. At dusk owls rise from their daytime roosts and begin to hunt. And at times the trees are swarming with warblers.

During the peak days of the migration you can see cars from every state in the parking lot near the Whitefish Point Bird Observatory headquarters, a facility operated by the Michigan Audubon Society. On the other side of the parking lot is the Great Lakes Shipwreck Museum, also busy though it attracts a different crowd. The last time we were there we followed a boardwalk past the museum and joined a small crowd on one of the wood-framed observation decks scattered throughout the grounds. With us were a few curious spectators and two or three others who seemed to have wandered there by mistake, but everyone else clearly knew their birds. Several of the most advanced of them were jostling for dominance. They stood out from the beginner birders, not just because of their expensive spotting scopes, but also because they never stopped scanning the sky. They were constantly alert, and when a bird appeared they identified it instantly.

Two of the experts, who appeared to be vagabonds, were men in their 30s who apparently knew each other from other birding destinations such as Brockway Mountain on the Keewenaw Peninsula. Both were scanning the sky to the south with battered spotting scopes mounted on tripods.

One of the men wore a hoody, had a well-scuffed water bottle hanging from his belt, and was quiet but authoritative. He would announce, "Merlin coming straight at us," and everyone would swing their binoculars in that direction.

The other guy was portly, quick-witted, very talkative, and didn't mind being the center of attention. As he scanned the sky he kept up a running account of his recent sightings. "Last week I was at Peshtigo," he said, "and saw a dozen Canadas in a field and in their midst was a snow goose. Then two days later a Ross' goose." His spoke loudly and rapidly. It was easy to imagine him holding court at a *Star Trek* convention. And he was incredibly sharp-eyed. "Here comes a peregrine, just above the tree line," he said, "coming fast and low." And we swung our binoculars in that direction and tried to spot it.

Gail and I are solid intermediate birders but we'll probably never advance much beyond that level. For one thing, we have poor ears for songs, so are limited mostly to the birds we can see. There's also our attention-span problem. We set out to go birding but can't cross a river without stopping and can't drive through a likely looking woods without stopping to search for morels. If we're in the mood for a little chaos and artifice, the casinos draw us in. And we have to check out every rocky beach for agates.

One of our favorite of those beaches is at the end of a long and deeply rutted two-track that appears on no maps. Last year when we were there Superior was in a rare tranquil mood, calm and steel-gray to the horizon, with tiny waves lapping the shore. We found a few smallish agates in the gravel and were bent over looking for more when, from a thicket of osiers at the top of the beach, came a distinctive, vaguely familiar call—"wickity wickity wickity." We were baffled for a moment, then remembered: the common yellowthroat, a warbler I've never for a moment thought was common.

Farther down the shore we came upon a number of logs half-buried in the sand. They were large—sixteen feet long and two feet in diameter—and worn smooth, the bark long gone, their wood bleached pale by weather. The ends of each were stamped with marks to identify the companies that owned them. Most of them were imprinted with the letters "OK." The others were simple heart shapes.

I remembered meeting a man who had worked as the skipper of a tugboat that hauled similar logs across Superior. He said they were cut far north in Ontario and hauled to the shore in trucks, then chained into booms the size of football fields. His job was to use his tugboat to push the booms along the north shore of the lake to the sawmills in Sault Ste. Marie, Ontario. He told a story about getting caught in a storm with wind and waves so powerful they shoved the raft of logs and his tugboat backward despite him running the tug's engine full throttle to fight it. They were pushed the entire width of Superior until they approached the Michigan shore and he had no choice but to abandon the boom and retreat to Canada. The boom eventually broke up, releasing its cargo of logs. Strays sometimes drift in the lake for years and are a hazard to small boats before sinking to the bottom or washing up on shore.

It was impossible to tell if the logs Gail and I found on the beach that day had been floating in the lake for months or for decades. Maybe they had been lost from a boom; maybe the very one the Canadian man had described. I imagined the storm that could shove a tugboat backwards against its thrusting propellers and break strong chains and scatter logs across hundreds of squares miles of water. If you've seen Lake Superior in a fury you'll have no doubt who wins such a contest. Tugs are powerful machines, but the smart money is on Superior.

The Night Country

Do you see Orion? Arcturus? Greek warriors strutting in a battlefield of stars?

I never do. I can't get past the stars themselves and the fact that they are the same stars watched in wonder by people a hundred thousand years ago. I see the vastness of space and vast swaths of time. Freud marveled that the unconscious mind, like the universe, is inexhaustible—an interior infinity to balance against the exterior one. Atoms and nebulae, galaxies and grains of sand: inexhaustible. We stand alone all our lives but never more alone than beneath the sky at night.

How do we understand a star that ceased to exist long before its light reached us—that flared and exploded or was sucked into a black hole billions of years before the first living creature walked the earth? We're seeing time, not matter. A pinprick of light that is time's echo, reverberating across the universe, like the spot on your retina after the flashbulb goes off. Fossil light. A memory of light. But one that is somehow just as real as the thing remembered.

Nights when I can't sleep I sometimes walk down the road to the bay and stand beneath the stars to think about time. The three-o'clock hour is best, when we're so deep into the night that the planet seems to have stopped spinning. The dew has fallen, the stars are at their brightest, the people in the neighborhood are asleep. The machinery of the earth is at rest.

The night sky is an excellent corrective to our self-importance. Everything superficial falls away. Vanity disappears. Politics, culture, and fashions fade to insignificance. It's just us, alone beneath the infinite, as we've been since the beginning.

If you're attentive, you can discover a new awareness of the land around you. There's something about seeing a place under changed conditions—in the morning after the first snowstorm of the season, in a rain shower, during the midday dusk of a solar eclipse—that awakens new appreciation. That's especially true at night. It becomes a different place altogether. The veil of familiarity peels away and all your senses are alerted. It's like stepping off an airplane into a foreign land.

You hear things you don't notice in daylight. The faraway moan of a truck downshifting on the highway. The hollow query of an owl. The cadence of night insects. Unfamiliar scents arise as well. The grass exhales a verdant musk, and the lake gives off trails of fragrance that can take you back decades.

When our sons were young Gail and I sometimes woke them late at night and led them outside to experience these wonders. There was a night when we were alerted by a phone call from a friend and went outside to see the most spectacular aurora of our lives. Swaying across the northern sky were red and green curtains so bright it was as if buckets of watercolor were streaming down the heavens. Another night we walked out in the field to witness a trio of rare events: the moon in full eclipse, Mars in conjunction with the moon, and the comet Hale-Bopp suspended in the sky and glowing faintly, like a flashlight under water.

Once we took the boys to an observatory. It was a moonless night, cold and without wind, and the stars were very bright. When it was my turn to look through the eyepiece I thought I knew what to expect, but I was wrong. It was the first time I had looked through a powerful telescope, so it took a few moments to realize that many of the pinpoints of light that I had always assumed were stars in our own Milky Way Galaxy, were, in fact, other galaxies. Then I started focusing on the spaces between those galaxies and saw other galaxies, progressively smaller and more distant, but so many of them that I realized that if the telescope were powerful enough we would see galaxies in every gap between every galaxy, all adrift with incomprehensively vast differences between them. I *felt* those distances and, for a moment, felt the vastness of the universe.

Tonight, as I write this, our first grandchild is being born. I'm already planning for the nights when I can lead her outside to see the Milky Way strewn across the sky. We'll walk to the shore of the bay to watch the stars reflected on the water and to listen to the sounds the lake makes only at night. If she's in the mood to listen I'll tell stories, mythological ones and scientific ones and probably some invented ones as well. And I'll tell her what I know to be true: that she will stride with confidence across the world, that she will see wonders, that she will be mighty.

Rivers and Time

Even after a lifetime of paddling it still thrills me to make the first stroke with my paddle and feel the canoe leap ahead and meet the current. There's no better way to learn a river. You can learn it in a kayak, I suppose, but I prefer canoes. I like the extra cargo capacity and I appreciate the perspective that comes with sitting above the water rather than in it. And I like the tradition.

There's a hidden stretch of river not far from my home that offers decent fishing in every season. You can hike to it if you don't mind ruining a day trying to bust through a couple miles of swamp thicket. I did it once in March, when I figured the swamp would be frozen and easy to walk across. It wasn't. My snowshoes kept getting tangled in the tag alders, so I took them off and strapped them to my backpack, which already bulged with waders and fishing gear. After a few hours of plunging through ice and sinking to my knees in mud I finally reached the river but it was running too high to wade. I turned around and slogged back through the swamp and drove home.

In my canoe I can reach that same stretch of river in thirty minutes. And more often than not, even on summer weekends, I have it to myself.

When you paddle a canoe you become part of the history of the north country. For thousands of years native boat builders refined their bark and wood canoes to meet the requirements of northern rivers and lakes. Some of the boats were large, as long as 36 feet, and could carry a ton or more of cargo and could handle open water on the Great Lakes. Others were sleek and fast, designed to transport a war party a hundred miles in a day. Still others were small and nimble, for maneuvering in fast rivers. Today's canoes, even those made of synthetic materials and aluminum, are built on the same principles of hull shape and proportion as the bark canoes of the Ojibwa.

Canoes are a perfect fit for our waters. We're lucky, here in Michigan, that the law declares any stream large enough to float a log is open to use by every citizen. In a canoe or kayak you can travel those rivers untaxed and unregistered, as free as anyone can be in this world of increasingly complicated impediments and encumbrances.

We're lucky also to have so many waters to choose from. I've explored rivers across much of the U.S. and Canada and on a couple other continents as well, but Michigan's will always be my favorites. And not only the sand-and-gravel streams of the northern Lower Peninsula, where I grew up. I'm fascinated with the variety of rivers everywhere on both peninsulas. We have wide rivers and skinny ones, rivers that flow a few miles between lakes and others that you can follow for a couple hundred miles, camping as you go. There are slow-running rivers stained dark with tannins; gravel-bottomed riffle-and-pool streams as clear as spring-water; and furious whitewater rivers that are among the most challenging in the Midwest. Some flow through the wildest forests in the state and others through the hearts of our cities. They meander across agricultural lands, through lowland forests and upland forests, down rock-strewn canyons. We have rivers to match every level of paddling experience. And each of them will take you to places you might otherwise never see.

Paddling is one of the best ways I've found to escape ordinary life. It's such an effective antidote to our everyday obligations and responsibilities—and to the tyrannies of superhighways, airports, and the 24-hour news cycle—that I think of it as a form of social protest. There's something so timeless about it that it can make you forget time altogether.

A Bountiful Weekend

Friday we played hooky to go birding at Sleeping Bear Point. We'd heard a few days earlier that it had been the site of what birders call a "warbler dump," with hundreds of migrating warblers dropping into the aspen thickets on the dunes to rest before crossing open Lake Michigan to the next landfall. They were trapped there by a north wind and by squadrons of circling raptors. One guy said on social media that every time a bluejay flew into the aspens it panicked half a dozen warblers into flight, where they were picked off by swooping merlins and sharp-shinned hawks. We wanted to see this for ourselves so we got up early enough to be there before dawn.

But when we got to the dunes the wind was blowing strong and very cold, and in two hours of searching we saw no warblers, though we might have heard a yellow-rump singing. Later we would learn that while we were shivering in the dunes another warbler dump occurred 150 miles north, at Whitefish Point.

We left Sleeping Bear and drove to a park on Little Glen Lake where we saw, in thickets of red osier, a Wilson's warbler, a redstart, and a yellow warbler. Then we continued south, stopping now and then to scope the trees for birds or to pick ditch asparagus.

At Otter Creek birds were everywhere: alder flycatcher, common yellowthroat, chestnut-sided warbler, a green heron. On impulse we walked into the woods to a cluster of ash trees that had not yet been killed by the emerald ash borer infestation and found twenty white morels at their base. I looked around at the mixed, mature hardwoods and started thinking about ovenbirds. They're one of my favorite songbirds, but are relatively scarce; we see only one or two most years. I like their chicken-walk strut, how they kick the leaf-litter in search of bugs as if they own the woods. They're not like other warblers. I said out loud, "This would be a good place to see an ovenbird," and we walked twenty yards over a small rise and there was an ovenbird below us, kicking leaves.

Saturday we worked, because I suppose one has to make a living. Sunday Aaron and Chelsea arrived with their pop-up camper and set it up in the backyard. Nick joined us, and the five of us hiked to a favorite woods to search for mushrooms. We found many. It was a bumper year. Spring had arrived late and the morels were two weeks behind schedule. It had been cold most of April and half of May, then came three days of warm, soaking rain, chased by another cold front. Apparently the rain brought the mushrooms up and the cool weather preserved them.

We drove to another secret spot and found more morels. While searching in a wooded valley that has long been one of our most reliable mushroom spots, we nearly stepped on a tiny spotted fawn, one or two days old, curled on the ground and watching us without fear. We backed off and went in another direction. Chelsea gathered a double handful of wild leeks with bulbs the size of my thumbs. The stems and leaves were starting to turn yellow and collapse, a stage I always assumed meant the bulbs were too tough and grub-infested to be edible. But they turned out to be delicious skewered with summer squash, cherry tomatoes, and shrimp, drizzled with olive oil, and cooked over the grill.

I don't know how many miles we walked that day, but when we finally got back to the car nobody could muster the energy to talk. When the silence lingered too long, I said, "Looks like we walked all the silliness out of us."

Aaron brightened and said, "Not me . . ." but he was too tired to think of anything silly to say.

That evening our neighbors, Andy, Andrea, and their young daughter, Alison, joined us for dinner. I put chicken on the grill next to Chelsea's kabobs, Aaron made mushroom miso soup, and Nick fried a couple pans of morels tossed in flour and fried in butter and served them as appetizers. After dinner we built a fire in the backyard firepit and sat around it roasting smores and telling stories. I told one about an aurora display that we had seen ten years earlier that was so brilliant some people thought they were seeing a distant forest fire and called 911. Young Alison begged her parents to let her stay up late to watch for the Northern Lights, but they had to get up early the next morning to drive to Chicago.

Maybe it's my age, but lately I've been appreciating temporary things. Time with the ones we love. Insects of the order Ephemeroptera. Lightning storms over Lake Michigan. The glimpses we're granted now and then of something we can only call radiance.

Our bountiful weekend came and was gone in a flash, but we were fine with that. It's the way all the best things go.

The Dawn Chorus

Morels usually start popping in early or mid April around here, but the big white ones don't show up until May. You can find them hidden in the high grass along roadsides or standing proud near the trunks of ash and apple trees. Some years we find them in our backyard, which seems like a benediction. Once my sons and I collected an onion-sack full behind John and Peggy's house next door. They live most of the year in London and don't mind if we forage on their property.

But morels are just one of our spring rituals. Mayflies are hatching. Trout are feeding. Flocks of birds are passing through. The vegetable gardens need to be planted. The challenge is deciding what to do— garden, fish, forage, or look for birds? It's the fox-in-the-henhouse dilemma. If you're like me (and the fox), your impulse is to grab all the chickens at once. Why not? As the great Kinky Friedman once said, "Find what you love and do it until it kills you."

The first day of May this year I woke at daylight to the sound of birdsong fluting from the treetops. The dawn chorus! Songbirds around the world are in decline, making their songs more bittersweet every year. They're victims of the dark side of the Anthropocene: a warming planet, habitat destruction, irresponsible overuse of pesticides and herbicides. Those of us who don't want to live in a world without birdsong are doing our best to remain hopeful.

That morning it was a little easier than usual to have hope. I'd been lashed to my desk for months working to satisfy my inner Puritan taskmaster, and now I needed to bust free. First I drove to a secret creek I hadn't fished in years. At the bridge I hiked through cedar swamp dense enough to discourage all but the most determined humans until I came to a stretch of creek latticed with fallen trees. I rigged my spinning rod with a hook and split shot, baited it with a garden worm, and crawled on my hands and knees to get into position.

Carefully I lowered the bait into a plunge pool the size and depth of a bucket. Instantly I felt a rap-rap-rap and hoisted an eight-inch brookie from the water. It was jade-colored and spotted with rubies. I had promised myself I would bring trout home for dinner but as usual I couldn't bring myself to kill such a beautiful creature. I unhooked it gently and cradled it in the current. Instantly it gave a kick and darted away.

Next I drove to a favorite mushroom woods, hung my binoculars around my neck, and set out on foot through the trees. I found no mushrooms but saw a yellow-throated vireo, my first ever, then stood for an hour on an open rise above the pines and watched groups of mixed warblers pass through in pulses, a dozen or two in each group, the birds hopping and fluttering from branch to branch, always making their way north. They moved too quickly to be easily identified, but I saw yellow-rumps and palms, a few yellows, a black-and-white, and a black-throated-green.

And so the day went.

It's the middle of January as I write this and I'm at my desk trying to be industrious when all I want to do is throw a few things in the car and drive south until I meet spring head-on. It might be along the Gulf Coast or in Florida, I don't care, I'll drive as far as necessary. And when I find the place where trees are bursting into leaf and birds are singing their hearts out and wildflowers are in bloom, I'll turn my car around and surf the season north fifteen miles a day until I'm home.

Summer

Summer and Slow Time

Suddenly it's summer—and not just the season of blue skies and verdant woods, of songbirds in the morning, thunderstorms in the afternoon, and fireflies at night, but the languid respite from responsibilities and schedules that we remember so fondly from childhood. Then as now it can seem timeless, lazy, as far removed from the productive seasons as the apple orchard is from the office.

For a few years when I was very young my parents thought that summer should be for taking vacations to ocean and mountains, to Chicago or New York or Disneyland. But after one or two trips my brother and I dug in our heels in protest. Why would we want to leave Michigan in the summer? Our house was on an inland lake; we had a dock, a rowboat, a powerboat, a pontoon raft anchored over the drop-off. We wanted to spend our summers fishing and waterskiing and camping on the island with our friends. Twenty miles away was Lake Michigan with its endless sand beaches and surging schools of salmon, and within bicycle range were ponds full of bluegills and woods laced with trails and cedar swamps where the creeks were alive with brook trout. There was canoeing, swimming, baseball, and playing with our dog. Who could bear to miss even a day of that? Early in the mornings Rick and I could slip from the house and stay lost until dark. We were explorers of the near at hand, world travelers who never had to leave home. It was everything a boy could want.

Or that a man could want. For I have changed little after all these years. I still prefer to stay in Michigan in summer, still spend as many days as I can in the woods and on lakes and rivers, searching for walleyes and warblers, for wildflowers and champion trees, for ruffed grouse and brook trout.

Summer is the high season for down-and-dirty adventures. It's the best time to explore those small, overlooked sanctuaries that time hardly alters—the blueberry bog and the tree-shaded pond and the pine forest where the floor is softer than any carpet. It's the season for wet shoes and sweat-stained hats, for wearing a canteen on your belt and consulting your compass even if you know where you are. It's the season for rediscovering the kid you used to be.

Getting Lost

Here's what turns my crank: free-flowing rivers in wild country, ponds hidden in tamarack swamps, campsites under white pines swaying in a breeze, trout gulping mayflies. I like pushing off in a canoe. I like slinging a heavy backpack onto my shoulders. I like knowing that if I find a woods or a pond or a stretch of river that suits me I can stay there for a few days or a week. And I like going my own way, at my own pace, and stumbling upon beautiful and interesting places.

So of course I like northern Michigan. After a lifetime of exploring it, my appreciation just keeps growing.

For one thing, we're never more than a few miles from water here. And with so much of the two peninsulas protected by state and national forests there are thousands of miles of trails to explore. The opportunities for adventure are endless, and you don't need to go far to find it.

On summer weekends Gail and I like to throw some gear in the back of the car, strap our canoe to the racks, and head for the woods. We take our time and drive the trails slowly, with the windows open, so we can spot berry bushes and smell sweet fern and more easily catch glints of water through the trees. On the seat between us we keep our water-stained and dog-eared book of county maps open so we can make notes in the margins—"Good bluegill lake," "Grouse cover along this creek, 2019," "Many blueberries here, 2016."

If you're inclined, you can crank up the investigation further by going online. One approach that has paid dividends for me is to access the DNR's database of fish stocks. There you'll find listed every lake and river in Michigan that has received plantings in the last thirty years, as well as the township coordinates of the planting sites. So if you're heading to Kalkaska County, for example, and want to find Lake Whimsy, which receives about 3,000 brown trout a year, you can enter the coordinates into your GPS.

Not that you have to be that scientific. It's just as easy and often more satisfying to head to the woods with no plan at all. Or maybe just follow your hunch that in the big country north of the highway are some places you'd like to explore and some two-tracks that might get you there.

In a radius of fifty miles from our home are more streams, lakes, and ponds—and more forests, swamps, bogs, and dunes—than anyone could explore in a lifetime. There are birds and wildflowers to study, fish to catch, berries and mushrooms to gather. Meandering trails will lead us to them, and they can get us happily lost, too.

And isn't that the point? Get lost, so we can discover new places. Get lost, so we can forget about work and money worries and the latest political scandal. Get lost, so we can learn more about the places we love—and maybe learn a little more about ourselves, as well.

Island Song

On the seldom placid waters of Duncan Bay, all the young mergansers were scared stupid. Osprey, eagle, fox, wolf—every predator eats merganser chicks as if they're fluffy Doritos. But in my mind there was only one reason those manic fuzzballs skittered in panic across the bay: northern pike, big mothers.

Of course this was mostly wishful thinking. My wife and I had come to Lake Superior's Isle Royale to canoe and camp and fish for the giant pike we'd heard lived in the bays that ring the island. We knew that Isle Royale National Park, which includes the forty-five-mile-long main island and an archipelago of two hundred surrounding islets, was the least visited national park in the lower forty-eight states. We knew too that it contained some of the last unspoiled country in the Great Lakes region. This vestigial wilderness in our backyard had always loomed big, like a famous aunt in the family. But somehow we'd never taken the time to visit.

We arrived on a Sunday morning in July after a five-hour, fifty-four-mile crossing from Copper Harbor, Michigan, on the 81-foot-long *Isle Royale Queen III*, a ferry known affectionately by locals as "The Barf Barge" or "The Chuck Wagon." The lake when we left Copper Harbor was choppy—the skipper called it "bouncy"—with two-foot waves quartering from the southwest, but the farther we traveled from shore the bigger the waves became. A trio of middle-aged ladies dressed for a day at the country club spent most of the passage to the island puking over the transom. For three or four hours during the middle of the crossing, with no land in sight, the ferry climbed and plunged through waves five to six feet high. Each time the vessel dived into a trough it scooped gallons of water onto the canopy above the deck. When it climbed the next wave, the water on the canopy rushed to the stern and dumped a waterfall over the heads and backs of the earnestly vomiting ladies. They couldn't have been more miserable if they were being dragged behind with ropes.

By my informal count one in four passengers was seasick. I shared that information with a crew member.

"Sounds about right," he said in a cheerful voice.

"What about when the waves are bigger?" I asked.

"Then *everybody* pukes."

When you've lost sight of land on Superior, it feels as if you're balanced on top of a vast convex lens of blue water. There's nothing but water to the horizon in every direction. The sky bears down with a presence that feels like physical weight. You have the sense that the lake hasn't changed since the centuries when native people and voyageurs first dared cross it in bark canoes—and that it won't have changed much by the time the planet finally shakes us off her back for good. It remains what it has always been: a huge, powerful buffer against everything temporary and superficial.

The power of the lake is evident also on the land around it. The Superior shore is rugged, a land of shattered rocks and wild forests made wilder by the constant battering of waves and wind. As we came into view of the tiny natural inlet at Isle Royale's Rock Harbor I was reminded of my first view of Newfoundland from a ferry. Here were the same scalloped coves carved from bedrock. The same hills thick with spruce. The same few buildings clinging to the shore and made smaller and more tenuous by the immensities of water, forest, and sky around them.

On the dock at Rock Harbor, waiting for us as we disembarked, were two of the happiest park rangers in the world. They had the bright eyes and luminous smiles of people bolstered by One True Religion or bountiful trust funds, and they couldn't wait to tell us how lucky we were to be there. They seemed genuinely wounded when a few of our group displayed a lack of enthusiasm. The ladies who had passed the trip purging themselves wanted only a shower and a bed. They and others who had arrived planning on a day of golf and cocktails were looking around in bewilderment. There's a lodge in Rock Harbor with comfortable rooms and a restaurant offering a two-entrée per evening menu, and, hooray, adult beverages. But you'll find no golf courses or tennis courts on the island, no roads, no televisions, no internet. There are no public telephones either, and no bars on your cellphone. If you don't enjoy hiking, boating, fishing, birding, botanizing, or examining interesting stones, your days on Isle Royale can grow very long.

Gail and I set off immediately for the backcountry. It's not far. Thirty feet from the dock is a worn footpath linked to 165 miles of hiking trails. Moose sometimes stroll down to graze on the goldenrods growing around the park store. We carried our canoe and gear across a short asphalt trail and put in at Tobin Harbor. A half-mile paddle across the harbor is the portage trail to Duncan Bay, the first hard leg of any paddling trip on the island.

Our plan was to paddle and portage through the bays and islands around the northeast third of the island, then follow a string of interior lakes and trails that make it possible to complete a thirty-three-mile loop back to Rock Harbor. Most paddlers give themselves four to six days to complete the loop, though a pair of rangers told us with modest pride that they did it once on their day off in thirteen hours.

Our plan was sound, but we had arrived in the middle of a hot and windy spell. Anyone who visits Isle Royale has to be prepared for some wind, although probably not as much as we encountered. Rangers told us it was the windiest week of the summer so far. Waves pounded every shore, and the Big Lake was so warm that you could swim in water that most summers is too cold for all but the hardiest swimmers. Lake Superior is famously cold. Dangerously cold. The mean surface temperature in midsummer at mid-lake averages about 55 degrees Fahrenheit.

But in recent years it's been warming at an alarming rate. Researchers have determined that it is the fastest-warming large body of freshwater on the planet. During our visit the surface of the open lake was a balmy 65 degrees and in the bays it reached 75.

Riding the wind three miles down Duncan Bay, we studied the dynamics of wind and water at close range. It sounds like fun on the page, but it was mildly terrifying. The waves grew larger with every mile, from swells to steep whitecaps that underran us, lifting the canoe in surges, then dropping it two or three feet into each trough. We made good time, I'll admit that. But the swells caught the stern from behind and made the canoe want to yaw. Only by prying my paddle hard against each wave could I keep us from broaching. We were wearing our personal floatation devices and the water was warm, so capsizing would probably not be life-threatening. But we would have to swim the swamped canoe and any gear we could salvage to shore in those waves.

We flew the length of the bay, aiming for a spit of land that was the last safe landfall before the bay opened into Lake Superior. Out there was an imposing and seemingly endless expanse of big water exposed to the full strength of the wind. The waves out there were much bigger. They bucked and rolled against the horizon. We were so relieved when we finally plowed onto the gravel beach and pulled our canoe above the reach of the breakers that our knees wobbled. We set up camp in a raspberry patch littered with moose droppings.

After we were settled we walked along the shore and ran into a pair of optometrists from Bloomington, Minnesota, who had motored from the Minnesota shore in a twenty-foot runabout equipped with GPS and ship-to-shore radio and were camped a quarter mile from us on the beach. Even with a seaworthy vessel and state-of-the-art equipment it takes some brass to cross the open lake. Superior is almost as big as the state of Maine. When it storms, small boats blow away like leaves. We stood on a rocky point and talked fishing. Beyond us, out on the open lake, eight-foot swells rolled and tossed. Even here, in relative protection, the wind scythed the tops off whitecaps and flurried the water in cat's-paws as big as city blocks.

The optometrists said they'd been coming to the island for ten years to troll for lake trout and steelhead. They wore week-old beards and carried themselves like men who wrestle grizzlies for sport. It's an interesting phenomenon. I've seen it before. A place as wild and unspoiled as Isle Royale can make you so environmentally hyperconscious that you begin worrying about color pollution—should we have brought a green tent instead of an orange one? Or it can turn you into a barbarian. You spend fifty weeks a year selling fashionable eyewear in the Mall of America, then you come to Isle Royale, carry a knife on your belt for a couple days, and you're transformed into a poor-grammar-speaking, raw-meat-eating, whup-ass from Wildville.

I mentioned that Gail and I hoped to catch pike on our fly rods, from our canoe. One of the optometrists hawked and spit. "No friggin' way," he said.

"You might hook 'em," his buddy said, "but you ain't gonna land 'em. A few days ago we was trolling for lakers in the bay and a big pike grabbed my spoon. I didn't have a chance, not even with fifteen-pound test and a salmon net. I don't know how big he was. Over twenty pounds, for sure. Maybe thirty. Then he decided to run—boom, crash, adios motherfuckers. After that I was scared to throw another lure in the water. Hell, I was scared to put my hand in the water."

"Besides," the first guy said, "the water's too warm. All the pike have gone deep."

It took two days to reach Herring Bay, the jumping-off point for the open-water crossing to McCargoe Cove and entry to the heart of the island. From McCargoe, you paddle and portage through a series of lakes—Chickenbone, Livermore, LeSage, and Richie—then portage two miles to Moskey Basin. From there it's a ten-mile paddle down Moskey to Rock Harbor again. But we hadn't counted on the wind.

Herring Bay is approximately the halfway point and a critical junction if you plan to complete the loop. From there to McCargoe is a two-mile crossing of open water, along an unprotected rocky shoreline. Some days Lake Superior is so calm you could probably paddle to the mainland in a canoe. But usually not. Almost never. Now we were facing strong winds from the northwest, the worst possible direction. We would later learn that the wind had increased a little every day, to a steady 35 knots, gusting to 45. Even bays that were ordinarily protected were churning with whitecaps, and on the open lake waves ran to eight feet. Now waves detonated against our shore, launching spray to the treetops. A black squall line swept across the water toward us, spears of lightning stabbing beneath it. The lake roared. When Lake Superior roars you can hear it miles inland. It's no time to be out there.

You have to figure your chances of getting around the headland at McCargoe at about fifty-fifty. Elsewhere the odds are worse. The long exposed end of Blake Point, at the extreme northeast tip of the island, is perhaps the most treacherous spot. On a map it appears to be an inviting alternative to the portage between Tobin Harbor and Duncan Bay. All you have to do is paddle to the end of the bay, round the point, and enter another protected bay. Piece of cake.

Except Blake Point is exposed full-on to Lake Superior's fetch. Big rollers and frequent squalls blast the shore. A park ranger told us that more rescues are performed at Blake than anywhere on the island. If you're lucky, maybe one day (or, more likely, one dawn) out of twelve is calm enough to allow a small open boat to pass safely around it. The rest of the time you're toast. If you swamp you get trashed on the rocks, and that's the least of your worries.

After hearing about the hazards of Blake Point we decided the portage at Duncan Bay wasn't so bad after all. The first time over it was difficult because we were carrying enough food for two weeks. A week later we would know what to expect and would be a few pounds leaner and a few degrees meaner than before. We trotted across, like bad-ass voyageurs.

At Herring Bay we made camp in an alcove in the balsams, with a view across fifteen miles of water to the Ontario shore. Thunder Bay indented the horizon, and the Sleeping Giant, a mountain of vaguely human shape considered holy by the Ojibwa, rose in the smoky distance. According to legend, the mountain contained silver mines given to the Ojibwa by the deity Nanabijou, who promised that any white men who learned of its location would be killed. One day an Ojibwa man betrayed his people and led white profiteers to the mine. But when their canoes neared the Sleeping Giant a sudden storm swept across the lake and all were drowned.

We waited three days while Lake Superior threw its tantrum. While we waited we explored. For such remote terrain, Isle Royale has a rich human history. The portage trail beside our camp had probably been used for at least 4,500 years, first by ancient copper miners who left shallow-pit mines scattered across the island, and later by white trappers, fishermen, miners, and loggers intent on wringing as much profit from the place as possible. The island has been the subject of enough scientific research to sustain a small university. Biologists crisscross the trails and waterways and use aerial surveys to study wolves and moose, monitor the loon population, net and tag coaster brook trout, check amphibians for environmental stress.

Early in the 20th century a half-dozen resorts and lodges promoted Isle Royale as a getaway for the well-heeled. Developers bought swaths of shoreline and built clay tennis courts and miniature golf courses until 1931, when a few far-thinking people succeeded in lobbying for national park status. Since then the island has reverted to something like its natural state, though wilderness devotees dislike the daily use fee and the strict camping regulations and are disappointed to learn that they must share the island with maybe two hundred people on any given day in summer.

But of course two hundred people should be able to share a space ten times the size of Manhattan, especially when most of them are camped at Rock Harbor or enjoying the spartan amenities of Rock Harbor Lodge. In a week of camping and paddling during the peak of the tourist season, Gail and I encountered just a dozen people.

You soon realize that though Isle Royale is not true wilderness, wildness rules. Frequent fogs nurture beards of moss on every branch and trunk and give sustenance to the thickets of ferns and the thimbleberries that clog the understory and the lichens that paint the rocks. A few steps in from shore is plant growth so lush it rivals rain forests for impenetrability. It's a place that discourages bushwhacking. Moose sign is everywhere, from the piles of droppings on every trail to the pie-sized footprints marching across every bog and the silt bottoms of every shallow bay. Though the moose population fluctuates, in late 2020 there were about 1,800 of them, so it's common for backcountry visitors to spot at least one.

Less easily seen are the island's apex predators. Wolves first arrived
in the winter of 1948–49, crossing an ice bridge from Ontario, and
immediately began preying on moose that until then had been limited
in number only by available food. In the last half century, the wolf-
moose relationship on Isle Royale has been among the most carefully
studied in wildlife annals. In recent years the wolves have declined in
number, probably due to inbreeding and the loss of genetic variation,
and researchers fear they may be sliding toward extinction on the
island. At last count only fourteen remained, divided into three packs.
Each pack roams a territory of about three hundred square miles. They
take care to avoid human contact. When I asked a ranger what chance
we had of seeing one or even hearing one howl, he said, "Almost zilch."

We broke camp finally, beaten by the wind, and retreated from Herring
Bay to the long, sheltered finger-bays to the east. Mornings and evenings we hiked beaches and the backs of rocky promontories, paddled
protected waters, and cast Dahlberg Divers the size of whisk brooms.
While I fished, Gail, bless her heart, paddled. She maneuvered us parallel to shore, sculling to hold the canoe steady against the wind. I cast
a thousand casts and never caught a fish. The optometrists were right.
All the big pike had vanished. But one day we found where their offspring lived.

At the foot of one of the finger bays is a creek entering through a
marshy slough. The water is too shallow for powerboats, but in a canoe
or kayak you can push through the lily pads and paddle upstream until
you meet gentle current. A few hundred yards farther the streambed
begins to deepen and grow narrow until it is barely wide enough for
a canoe. Still we pushed on, going deeper into the bush. Where tag
alders formed a canopy overhead and the banks brushed the sides
of the canoe, we chanted "Hey Moose, hey Moose," to avoid surprise
encounters—when startled, cows with calves can be dangerous. At
one point we stopped so Gail could photograph wildflowers. The spot
was opulent with flora that rose in heaps and mounds around us and
spilled over the banks to the water. I held the boat steady while Gail
leaned forward, zoomed, focused, and shot. It was a nice moment. The
last thing on my mind was carnage.

For the hell of it, after Gail finished with the camera, I turned around in my seat and cast a big deer-hair popper a couple rod lengths downstream, to where the creek widened slightly at a dogleg and the current appeared to undercut the bank. The fly touched the water and tripped some kind of fiendish booby trap. Something vicious launched from the bank, ripped the creek apart, and devoured water, air, and popper in a ravenous gulp. My leader drifted back unadorned. Gail screamed as if she'd witnessed a murder.

"Cripes," I said.

"Try again."

"I'm not sure I want to."

I tied on another popper—first attaching a length of forty-pound-test monofilament as a shock tippet—and cast again. The pike—almost certainly the same two-footer—slaughtered the bug, felt the hook, and went insane. It slammed from bank to bank until it was exhausted. I grasped it behind the head and lifted it into the canoe and it went insane again. When it finally calmed and lay panting on the bottom of the hull I inserted pliers into its mouth and instantly it clamped down, like a dog on a pork chop.

We caught baby pike all the way back to the bay. The biggest was maybe twenty-six inches long. Not a trophy, but on surface flies and a six-weight rod it was fun. Maybe "baby pike" is the wrong term. These babies had malevolent eyes, and teeth designed to eviscerate. Play coochie-coo with them and they'd try to eat your fingers. Most people think of fly fishing as a gentle sport, lyrical and contemplative. But that's for trout. Fly fishing for pike is like playing hot-potato with fragmentation grenades.

The giant pike eluded us. Locals say a good time to try is late May, when the northerns lie like alligators in the shallows waiting for something stupid to blunder past.

The moose eluded us, too, which surprised the rangers back in Rock Harbor. They suggested we were unlucky, but we didn't feel unlucky.

Our last night we stayed in an Adirondack shelter at the foot of Duncan Bay. The shelters are the Holiday Inns of the backcountry, raised plywood structures with shingled roofs and screened fronts and cast-iron fire grills. Waterproof, bug-proof. All the comforts of home. We settled in, spread our sleeping bags, hung our gear from nails on the wall, read the graffiti. At sunset we paddled over the water where giant pike were said to roam but didn't and watched young mergansers sprint across the surface in fear of just about everything. Then we went to bed and slept the good sleep of the virtuous.

In the night we woke half-dreaming to music: bell-clear, chiming music that filled the space around the stars, songs of unspeakable sorrow, of loss and loneliness and mystery from times before language. I swam to consciousness, Gail prodding me with her elbow. We lay listening. There was only silence. We tried to remember what we had heard, but it had ended before we were fully awake and now we couldn't be sure what it was. Not coyotes; none live on the island. Maybe loons. Maybe waves. Maybe breeze strumming the boughs. Maybe nothing.

"Wolves," Gail whispered.

The Wind on the Beach

When the wind is up on Lake Michigan—and the wind is often up—Point Betsie can be a quieting place. I don't mean that it is without noise, for on this point of land, exposed to three of the four quarters of the wind, there is much wave clamor and wind howl. I mean it quiets us. Even when we're determined to make ourselves heard, we have little say in the matter. The wind outshouts us every time.

In my childhood Point Betsie marked the southern boundary of our home turf. My family and I spent many days exploring the beaches from there to Platte Bay and around Sleeping Bear Point to Glen Arbor. In late August and into September my father, mother, brother, and I fished for salmon in Platte Bay, sometimes trolling as far as Point Betsie but never beyond it. Like countless lake-farers before and since, we relied on the point and its lighthouse as a landmark. From a few miles offshore we could triangulate the lighthouse with the flank of Sleeping Bear and the notch in the forest where the Platte River entered the lake and know where to begin setting our lines. And like so many others before us, we took comfort knowing the beacon of the lighthouse was there if we needed it.

In those days, a few hours on the open lake was enough for me. I loved to fish but was always glad when we beached the boat at midday and went ashore to eat lunch and explore. After storms, especially, the beach held treasures: brightly colored fishing lures lost by fishermen, beach glass and Petoskey stones, maybe the desiccated carcass of a salmon or drowned monarch butterflies that had flown too close to the water and been snatched by waves. I followed the narrow trails through the marram grass with its razor edges, to protected swales hidden behind the dunes and sun-warmed interdunal ponds where I could wade in search of frogs and turtles. Farther in were dense island-like thickets of spruce and aspen where songbirds flitted in the shadows.

The dunes that line much of the eastern shore of Lake Michigan form the largest system of freshwater dunes in the world. That they have been under siege is no secret. They have been built upon, excavated into harbors, bulldozed level to make room for condominiums, and mined for sand that is used to cast engine blocks and other products. Many of the dunes at the southern end of the lake were long ago shoved aside to make room for industry, most dramatically for the steel mills of Gary and South Chicago, many of which have since failed, leaving a wasteland of rusting desolation in their place.

A different kind of desolation threatens the dunes up the shore in Michigan, though with equally irreversible consequences. People want to live on the water—who can blame them?—and many miles of former dunes have been sacrificed to make way for summer homes and cottages situated to take best advantage of the sunset view.

It's to our credit that some of the most beautiful dunes and shoreline have been preserved in state and national parks and other public ownership. We're fortunate, for instance, that the Zetterberg family from California began purchasing land at Point Betsie in 1927 and in 1988 donated some 70 acres of virgin dunes and shoreline to the Nature Conservancy. If the property had been put on the open market, it would surely have stirred a frenzy of development. Beachfront developments packed with condominiums and townhouses are the steel mills of the north, and land speculators are the titans of industry. The land would have been closed off for the benefit of a few, and a landscape unique in the world, along with the plants and animals that evolved over millennia to live there, would have been lost.

Because of the foresight of the Zetterbergs, this section of shore and dunes has changed little in more than half a century. But that is not to say that it is untouched. On a June morning, John Legge, the Conservation Director of the Nature Conservancy's West Michigan office, and Lara Rainbolt, Conservation Assistant and Office Manager, led Gail and me on a hike through the dunes and along the shore of the Zetterberg Preserve. They showed us first the work the Conservancy has done in conjunction with volunteers from AmeriCorps, under Lara's supervision, to control the invasive plant known as baby's breath. An innocuous-seeming plant of the genus Gypsophilia (meaning "sand-loving"), it is native to the shores of the Black Sea and, when dried, is similar in appearance to the tumbleweed of the southwest deserts. It is frequently used in floral arrangements and is often bound into bunches and offered for sale. But this "pernicious nuisance species," as John Legge called it, has a powerful and deep-reaching taproot and the habit of profuse seeding, characteristics which allow it to get a firm grip in an ecosystem and dominate it, crowding out native plants. Point Betsie is thought to be home to the source population of baby's breath in the Great Lakes region, where it was probably first planted to be used in the floral trade. Its seeds, carried north and east by the wind, accumulate against forest walls and the lee sides of dunes and bluffs. The plant is migrating northward, making inroads into Sleeping Bear Dunes National Lakeshore and as far away as Petoskey, about 100 miles north.

As we stood in a swale dominated by the invasive plant, John Legge explained that until a selective herbicide is perfected the only way to control it is through "grunt work." He demonstrated how to drive the flat blade of a shovel deep into the sand until it nudged against the side of the taproot, then shoved his heel against the blade and sliced through the rutabaga-like root. "One down," he said. "A couple million to go."

Nearby was a pair of monitoring plots, their 10-meter boundaries marked with lengths of PVC pipe driven into the sand. Since 1990 researchers have studied the plots to learn what effects baby's breath, spotted knapweed, and other invaders have on native plants.

John and Lara then gave us a mini-course on forest succession—the ways that bearberry, creeping juniper, and mosses naturally stabilize the backdunes and eventually give way to boreal pockets of spruce, fir, and pine. Closer to shore they identified other natives: hoary puccoon, wormwood, broom rape, marram grass.

"Here's one you might find surprising," he said, kneeling to point at a small clump of grass. "Little bluestem." When I asked if it was the same grass that once thrived in such abundance on the prairies, he confirmed that it was and added that dunes and prairies share an "ecological affinity."

The dunes around Point Betsie are parabolic, named for their boomerang shape, and appear to roll, like ocean swells, inland from the lake. They lack the dramatic size of the high perched dunes farther up the shore at Sleeping Bear, which sit atop ancient glacial moraines. Parabolic dunes form on unstable sand, and thus are in constant migration and are subject to frequent blowouts. Scattered among them are wetlands and ponds, where a greater diversity of plants and animals can be found than elsewhere in the dunes.

We kneeled to examine specimens of Pitcher's thistle, a threatened species that remains abundant in the Zetterberg Preserve. The thistle is vulnerable because it requires two to eight years to mature before blossoming for a couple weeks in a single summer, then dying and scattering its seeds in a close circle around it. Evolved to live only in Great Lakes dunes, Pitcher's thistle is at risk from shrinking habitat and human foot traffic. We stepped carefully as we made our way among the thistles, and I couldn't help noticing the deep footprints we left in the sand, along with those of the people who had been here before us.

There's little chance that this popular preserve along the Lake Michigan shore will ever be free of such footprints. I'm not sure it should be. We need small wild places where the wild can exist side by side with the civilized. For most of Western history we've insisted that nature and culture are opposites, separated by clear boundaries. But in places like Point Betsie the boundaries blur. And that's good. The boundaries should blur. They're porous, after all. Examine them up close and you can see that there's no clear distinction between the natural and artificial, between inside and outside, between self and world.

When the wind is up at Point Betsie you can watch whitecaps charge the shore, each wave as it enters the shallows rising, growing steeper, reaching a peak, and throwing itself roaring onto the beach. That roar is the sound of the earth being changed. One of the wonders of the place is that it is constantly changing, while changing very little at all.

Sandblasted

We spent the night with our friends Betsy and Eric in a cottage they had rented on the shore of Lake Michigan near Point Betsie. The cottage was a 1950's-era Cape Cod perched on a dune a pebble toss from the waves breaking on the beach. The lap siding was old enough to have been sandblasted smooth and worn to the color of driftwood, and even the furniture inside seemed to have been roughly polished by sand. There was a fireplace in the living room and an intimate kitchen where two people could work together if they didn't mind bumping elbows. I do most of the cooking at home, but that evening at the cottage I was content to sit with Eric on the deck outside and drink wine and watch the sun going down while the women prepared dinner. Later Eric and I would do the dishes, but first we would have to wipe the counters with a damp rag to get the sand off.

It was a hot evening so Gail and I left the window open in our upstairs bedroom when we went to bed. Late in the night, around two a.m., I was awakened by flashes of lightning and detonations of thunder. I sat up and discovered that the wind had come up strong and was blowing a fine mist of rain through the screen. I kneeled in front of it and let the mist coat my face while I watched the waves breaking below. Whitecaps give off a lot of light. I hadn't realized how much. Then lightning flashed offshore and for a moment the entire lake was visible. It was chaos out there. Waves rushed toward us in trains, their white tops streaming like banners and horses' manes. They fell and burst into froth and rushed to the foot of the dune below the window. It felt precarious to be there, in that little cottage balanced on the sand, with the waves threatening to wash it away.

I went downstairs and found rain spraying through screens on every window, even on the lee side of the house. The roof was leaking, too, and puddles had collected on the hardwood floor in the living room. I shut the windows and searched the kitchen for pans to catch the dripping water and towels to sop up the puddles. Then I sat in a chair by the front window and watched the storm some more.

In the morning the four of us sat on the deck drinking coffee while looking at the lake. We laughed about how easy it is for water and sand to infiltrate a house. The storm had moved inland by then and the clouds were in tatters. The wind had diminished, but not by much, and waves still pounded the shore. Each breaker struck with a sonorous thump that we could feel through our feet. Betsy said her secret ambition was to spend every day for the rest of her life on the shore of Lake Michigan.

I asked her why.

"For the drama," she said. "I'm a sucker for the drama."

Our Bay Life

So I've become a homebody. Nobody is more surprised than I. But if you saw my home, you'd understand.

You'd understand especially in summer, for it seems that everyone wants to be in Traverse City in the sweet season. Can you blame them? Days on the bay and the inland lakes, evenings downtown at theaters, breweries, bookstores, restaurants. We even have a nightlife now—one that doesn't necessarily involve a bonfire on the beach and the hex hatch on the Boardman.

Summer's brevity only makes it sweeter. Our nightlife and daylife blend then, and our swimsuits never quite dry. The days are long but there are so few of them that we get a little boisterous from trying to pack so much into them. One summer we got especially boisterous with our son Aaron and his beautiful wife, Chelsea, she with the middle name "Bay," a grace note bestowed by her parents Mike and Carey Wills in honor of Grand Traverse Bay, this place so central to their lives. Chelsea's grandfather was Warren Wills, who lived down the hill from us on East Bay, in a house where Chelsea and her sisters spent part of every summer since they were old enough to swim. The bay has permeated the Wills and Dennis families for generations.

But these are golden years, too, and we never forget how fortunate we are to live here. When family or friends are visiting—the guest-room taken, the backyard a campground, the refrigerator stuffed with food, the wine rack full and the conversation and laughter unstoppable—we sometimes need to step away to be alone long enough to acknowledge how lucky we are. There are moments in summer, especially in the evenings, when the temperature outside and the temperature in the house are both about 80 degrees and we're sitting on the patio, in the breeze, in our bathing suits, when the image of cornucopia comes to mind. Life's abundance, overflowing.

The summer after Chelsea and Aaron got married they camped for several weeks in our backyard. Nick was living in Montreal or he would have been there also. Our kids can do their work anywhere, on laptops and smartphones, for their generation has made the world their office. We gathered intermittently throughout the day to shoot baskets in the driveway, identify bird songs, or walk to the shore to check the status of swash marks and Pitcher's thistle. Evenings we swam at the Linsells' beach, then cooked together and dined at our patio table looking over the bay.

Other adventures were for the weekends: Birding and picking wild berries at the point; sailing with Mike and Carey on West Bay while the sun dipped below the hills of Leelanau; paddling canoes from Haserot Beach and riding the pushy waves north until we'd gone just far enough to make it back to the car before dark.

Our bay life is about more than just water, of course. It's about the work we do (though that is often about the water as well). It's about the foods we enjoy—many of them grown and raised by our neighbors— and the rituals of gathering, preparing, and eating them. But especially it's about family and friends and our moments together: the laughter and music, campfires in the backyard, fishing trips and canoe outings, late nights under the stars. It's cornucopia, life's abundance spilling over—and summer's stern reminder to make every day count.

The Rules of Cottage Living

Not long ago I spent a year living in other people's cottages. There were nine of them in all, each on or very near the Great Lakes, extending from the Minnesota shore of Lake Superior in the west to the New York shore of Lake Ontario in the east. They varied from an 80-year-old log cabin, to a summer home so new that there was still sawdust and lumber scraps on the ground around it, to what can only be described as a mansion, but they shared a number of qualities. For example, they all had big windows facing the water, for the first rule of cottage living is that looking out the windows is the primary entertainment. This is unavoidable because the best cottages have no internet access or satellite TV, though many come stocked with a quirky assortment of movies on DVD or VHS and a beat-up player that sometimes works. Even so, standing at the windows watching water and weather will take up hours of every day.

The second rule of cottage living is that your sense of time needs to be adjusted.

That adjustment is gradual. It usually takes three days to break away from the pace of your ordinary life and remember how to relax. As the hours open up you'll probably have to get reacquainted with boredom. It's boredom, after all, that motivates you to set up the Monopoly board, shuffle the cards for cribbage and euchre, and refresh your memory with the copy of *Hoyle's Rules of Games* that is on a shelf somewhere in every cottage. Get bored enough and you'll finally read *The Rise and Fall of the Roman Empire* or *The Thorn Birds*, for cottage bookshelves are among our culture's great storehouses of floor-thumping books that we don't have the patience to read during our regular lives.

The third rule of cottage living is that everything there, every picture on the wall, every dish of Petoskey stones and beach glass, every dog-eared book and board game, comes saturated with memories.

Cottages are refuges from ordinary life, so almost by definition the time we spend there is extraordinary. Over the years the best moments from all those weekends and summers soak into the pine paneling and handwoven rugs and lumpy mattresses. If you listen carefully you can hear a generation or two of kids giggling in their bedroom while the grownups talk in low voices around the fireplace. You can sense what it was like during all those rainy days, with card games and checkers on the table, and always somebody stretched out on the couch reading a book.

The fourth rule, of course, is that it's your job to manufacture new memories.

The fifth rule: Get outside the minute the weather turns nice.

The sixth rule, and this one should be engraved on a board and hung beside the front door where everybody sees it twenty times a day: no lawnmowers!

A seventh rule comes to mind. This one was conceived by friends of ours, who emphasized that it was not popular. Not in the least. They said they waited to spring it on their kids until after they'd unpacked and settled into the cabin. Then they called a family meeting and announced that for the next two weeks on the shore of Lake Superior there would be no electronic devices allowed. None. Enforcement was easy—or, let's say, enforcement was possible—because they were in a place without cellular service. No Wi-Fi, either. Or television. The kids didn't know such places existed.

"It's a dead zone!" they cried. And cried. And cried.

"You would have thought it was the end of the world," my friend told me. "For two days and nights they went through all the stages of grief—shock, denial, anger, bargaining, depression. I thought I was going to lose my mind."

Then a strange thing happened. The kids discovered the beach out front. And they discovered that beyond the beach was a lake. And not just any lake. A lake so big that it disappeared over the horizon, as if it were an ocean. And breaking on the shore were waves that looked like they belonged on an ocean, too. And in the wash of the waves were heaps of colorful stones and pebbles they could gather and arrange in swirling patterns on the beach.

They saw birds they had never noticed—rafts of diving ducks riding the waves and, flying above them, terns that scanned the water constantly as they soared, now and then tucking their wings and plummeting into the water and a moment later emerging with minnows wriggling in their beaks.

They saw black squalls passing down the lake so far away that the shudders of lightning inside the clouds were silent. And at night the sky was filled with stars brighter than they had ever seen.

They learned how it felt to be confined indoors on a rainy day with nothing to do, when minutes could seem like hours and hours like days. And they solved that problem with Monopoly and Risk games they found in a cupboard, and with books they pulled from shelves in the living room. They discovered the pleasure of lying on a couch reading while rain finger-drummed the roof above them—and of falling asleep to that sound.

They discovered it was fun to sit at the dinner table telling stories to their parents and listening to the stories told in turn. Some of those stories were so funny and unexpected that they looked at their parents as if they had never seen them before.

It was all very strange. Time slowed and at the same time, somehow, expanded. For the first time, the kids paid attention to the sound of wind in trees. They noticed the scent of the lake—"It smells *big*," one of the kids said—and of the ferns and mosses in the woods behind the cabin.

None of them could believe how quickly those two weeks passed.

Sparks in the Sky

On summer days when I was a boy, my family and I often walked the shore of Platte Bay, from the mouth of the Platte River to Otter Creek. I remember one day in particular, in August of what must have been 1968 or '69, when the salmon were running and Dad was out in the boat fishing. Sleeping Bear Dunes were a hazy yellow mountain in the distance, and the lake was very blue. My mother, brother, and I walked barefoot, slapping our feet on the wet sand. Waves swelled and broke and washed high on the beach, then sank in a hissing of swash bubbles. I found an orange fishing lure lost by a salmon angler, and Mom spotted a five-dollar bill tumbling in the waves and waded in to retrieve it. We were treasure hunters, and Lake Michigan was overflowing with bounty.

In those days we often had the beach to ourselves. Many people still thought of the shores of the Great Lakes as undesirable—too cold, too windy, too plagued by blowing sand and biting insects and by the alewives that periodically died off by the millions and fouled the beaches. But my brother and I loved the shore just the way it was. To a kid, few places are more magical than an empty beach on a summer day.

The magic took many forms. We found drowned monarch butterflies, plastic toys washed pale of color, aluminum floats lost from the nets of commercial fishermen. There was driftwood shaped like herons and gazelles, and whole tree trunks worn smooth and faded silver by the sun. In the gravel were Petoskey stones and bits of beach glass as smooth as half-dissolved candy. Gulls and terns soared above us and pencil-legged sandpipers ran along the water's edge ahead of us. Often I would close my eyes and listen to the waves and be convinced that I could hear voices.

In the evenings my parents sometimes built a bonfire of driftwood on the beach and we would sit up late toasting marshmallows and watching meteors. After dark, Lake Michigan seems smaller, a lake rather than an inland sea. Some nights it is so calm that there are no waves at all. The stars then are equally bright on the water and in the sky, and you can sit next to the fire and watch sparks stream toward the Milky Way.

When there was wind I noticed that if I put my ear to the sand I could hear the impact of a wave breaking moments before the sound arrived through the air. Later I would learn that sound travels much faster through soil than air, but those nights I assumed I was hearing echoes or the thump of waves far down the beach. It was another mystery in a world filled with them.

Until you reach a certain age everything is amazing. Waves romp through the earth, sparks fly off to the stars, and if you listen very carefully you can hear voices in the water.

Ways of Seeing Sleeping Bear

The most beautiful place in America? You'll get no argument from me.

There are places that advertise their charms boldly. Some, like the Grand Canyon and Niagara Falls, slam you with spectacle. But the beauty of Sleeping Bear Dunes and the land and water that surround them is more subtle and grows deeper the more time you spend there. The closer you look, the more you'll see; the deeper you go, the more you'll discover. No wonder so many people are inspired by the place.

If you were lucky enough to know Sleeping Bear when you were a kid, as I did, your appreciation of the place probably goes very deep indeed. Some of my earliest memories are of playing with my brother and our cousins on the beaches at Empire and Glen Haven and of racing each other up the the Dune Climb. My mother grew up in a large family in Glen Arbor, so we were granted access to many secret places. We explored the beaches from the Platte River to Pyramid Point, hunted mushrooms in the woods, fished the inland lakes for bass and pike and the creeks and rivers for trout and salmon. When my brother and I were ten and twelve years old we filled our Boy Scout backpacks with enough supplies to gird us for the Sahara and hiked across the top of the dunes in search of buried treasure. We found ghost forests instead, and the remnants of a ghost village that would disappear in

1971 when Sleeping Bear Point slumped into Lake Michigan, and the ghost tracks of deer and bobcat, but no humans. We knew we had discovered a special place.

People must have always known it was special. They had been coming here for at least 8,000 years, and for many of the same reasons that we visit now. They came to hunt and gather berries and collect medicinal plants, to make maple sugar, to set up camps on points of land where the wind kept the mosquitoes away. There was magic in the place, and rich mythologies grew up around it.

Anyone who spends even a little time in Sleeping Bear National Lakeshore will recognize that some of that magic has its source in the great diversity of landscapes, water, and living things found here. Even the weather is more varied than in most places. There's something profoundly appealing about that. Take any of the trails on the mainland and North and South Manitou Islands and you'll pass through an array of landscapes. Some trails lead to dunes, part of the 300-mile network that stretches from Indiana to the Upper Peninsula, making it the most extensive freshwater dunes system in the world. Other trails pass through mature forests inhabited by dozens of species of trees and a profuse understory with twenty-five species of ferns and one-hundred or so wildflowers, including twelve varieties of orchid. So much of the park is wooded that it's a bit of a shock to break out into an open meadow that was hewn from the woods a century ago, abandoned when the sandy soil played out. You'll find bogs and other wetlands that are home to sixty types of sedges, and lakes, ponds, and streams where more than ninety species of fish live. Biologists have identified fifty mammals, twenty amphibians, eighteen reptiles, and more than two-hundred and forty species of birds in the park. Some of the birds are year-round residents, while others pass through only during their spring and fall migrations. Others, like the endangered Piping Plover and the threatened Prairie Warbler, nest here.

Naturally, all that diversity makes Sleeping Bear an irresistible subject for artists. The place is large enough and diverse enough to accommodate any eye, any medium, any style—and as a result the art that comes from it is often extraordinarily fresh. To get a better sense of any landscape—to *feel* what a place is like—we've always turned to art. I've seen Sleeping Bear Dunes countless times, yet I cannot walk past any artist's interpretation of it without experiencing a surge of excitement. The excitement is partly recognition of the familiar, but there's a thrill of novelty as well, as if I'm seeing the place for the first time. For of course each of us sees differently and every artist brings a unique set of experiences and knowledge to the work. This variety of perspectives gives us a truer and richer understanding of any subject, even one we thought we knew well. And we can take what we learn from artists back to the land and see it no longer as just sand, trees, and water, but as light and shadow, as color, as texture and shape.

Another reason Sleeping Bear is so interesting is that there are so many ways to experience it. We can get there on roads, in boats, on footpaths and ski trails. And although my own preference is to follow trails or bushwhack to the smallish, hidden corners of the park where the attractions might not be immediately evident, I'm as enchanted as anyone by the more popular places as well. Pierce Stocking Scenic Drive, with its series of overlooks, is a famous example. At each over-look you can park your car or bicycle and walk to platforms looking over the rolling dunes and swales at the top of the dunes. Turn inland and you'll see mile after mile of land that was shaped by the Pleisto-cene glaciers and is now rolling hills covered with forests, with gor-geous blue lakes nested among them.

There's a spot as you approach the Lake Michigan Overlook on the Stocking Drive that you shouldn't miss. It's not a secret, in fact it's hard to miss, but you need to keep your eyes open to get the full impact. The trail from the parking lot is steep, filled with loose sand, and leads past wind-twisted aspens to open dunes. When you crest the final bluff you're on an open dune perched 450 feet above Lake Michigan. And suddenly, there it is. The Big Lake. The whole world spread before you. Nothing but blue water and blue sky, all the way to the horizon.

Shorewalking

1.

In the spirit of Rousseau—"Man is born free, and everywhere he is in chains!"—I set out walking along the beach. During eight days in July I walked from Cathead Bay, near the tip of Leelanau County, to the village of Arcadia, in Manistee County, a distance of about sixty miles. I walked on private property and public, alone and in the company of friends, directed largely by whim, which of course is the only sensible plan for a beach walk.

The edges of the Great Lakes are among the last great places to go freely on foot, for as far as you desire. Where else can you walk mile after mile, day after day, and never cross a road? Our public lands are shrinking; some are becoming unsafe; many are unsuited for foot travel. But the Great Lakes, our vast interior commons, are ringed by more than ten-thousand miles of shoreline, much of it prime for walking.

Many of those miles are privately owned, which over the years has been the cause of a fair amount of controversy and a great deal of confusion. The Great Lakes themselves will always be too wild to be tamed, let alone possessed. But their shores are another matter. Where do we draw the line between property that belongs to everyone and property that belongs to a few? Especially when the property is bounded by waters so vast they defeat the very idea of ownership?

As it happened, I was walking on private beaches the very day that the Michigan Supreme Court ruled that I could rightfully do so. Before that day the law was hazy on the issue. Property owners assumed their ownership extended to the water's edge; beachwalkers argued that they should be allowed to pass through. The court settled the issue by mandating that everyone has the right to walk the shore of Michigan's Great Lakes beaches up to the ordinary high-water mark as long as they keep moving and do no harm. Never mind that the ordinary high-water mark is sometimes difficult to identify. Or that many people are still confused about the law. The strength of the ruling is its emphasis on common sense: Walk private shores if you wish, but stay close to the water, keep moving, and treat the land with respect.

I talked at some length about the issue with my friend Rich VanderVeen, who is founder and president of Mackinaw Power Company and a leader in the alternative-energy movement. The day that the Supreme Court made its decision, Rich and his son-in-law Dan Rutz had joined me to hike from Peterson Park to Cathead Bay. As we walked, Rich, who is a former attorney—or, as he says, a "recovering" attorney—tried to explain some of the finer points of usufruct.

When he noticed my eyes glazing over he bent and picked up a stick to use as a stylus. On wet sand near the water's edge he drew a line. "Here's the main thing you should know," he said. "At this end of the line is the private-property principle at its most extreme—the Three G's: God, Guns, and Gates—where owners can do anything they want with their land. At the opposite end of the line is public property, owned by everyone, accessible to everyone." He then marked several gradations between the two extremes, one of which, he said, was our right to walk on this particular beach despite it being private land. He straightened up, and a wave came in and washed his diagram away.

Dan noticed. He's an observant young man. He said, "And the lake gets the last word, as usual."

2.

Get a good pace going and you can feel your thigh muscles stretch and flex; dig your toes into sand and you become aware of tendons contracting all the way to your hips. There's something celebratory about knowledge rising through your feet into your blood, bones, and sinews. We learn the land by muscle memory.

Half a mile of it and you become convinced that you could walk your way to a new life. Stay in a chair at home and you won't change much. But get outside, place one foot before the other, and the doors of the world swing open. Pounds disappear, muscles grow toned, you become more alert.

Eventually you'll adjust your pace to the rhythms of the waves and the wind. You'll adjust your perspective, too. You might see the close view first: waves foaming up the wet beach and sinking into the sand, leaving swash bubbles bursting in tiny craters. Then you pull away and see the beach as it appears from above: a strip of yellow sand glaring in the sunlight, a clean boundary between the blue immensity of the lake and the dark hills that rise around it.

And, of course, you'll see the sun, the god of beach culture. We who live in the boreal forests of the northern Great Lakes region are woods dwellers. Our ancestors probably ran shrieking from the light. But the young couple I saw tanning naked on a blanket near North Bar Lake had the right idea. They were inviting the sun to drive away the demons that sneak in during winter's darkness and cold. I shut my eyes and turned my face to the sun and felt my skin sucking up hot doses of vitamin D. Too much is lethal, of course, so I wore my fishing hat and slathered on gobs of sunscreen.

Months later I found the notebook I carried on those days on the beach. I opened the water-wrinkled pages, held the paper to my nose, and inhaled the remnant fragrance of Coppertone. It took me instantly to Pyramid Point the day my wife, Gail, and I discovered, half-buried in the sand, a Petoskey stone as big as an office desk, its thousand eyes staring unblinking at the sun.

3.

In Platte Bay the beach is wide and slopes gently to low dunes covered with marram grass. When I was a kid cottages lined the dunes, but they were purchased by the park service long ago and have been removed. It remains one of the "secret" beaches within the park, which accounts for the large numbers of people who use it on summer weekends. The day I walked it, swimmers were keeping well clear of a swath of rotting algae that rose and fell with the waves. Here, as everywhere along Sleeping Bear Dunes National Lakeshore, people can walk anywhere they want. No private property issues to worry about.

I had wanted to learn more about the piping plover, the Great Lakes' most imperiled shorebird, so that day I invited Craig Czarnecki to walk with me to Point Betsie Lighthouse. Craig was then Field Supervisor for the U.S. Fish and Wildlife Service's Ecological Services Office, in charge of protecting federally endangered species throughout Michigan. The efforts of many people to protect the plover have been paying off. When they were first listed as endangered in 1986, only seventeen nesting pairs could be found in all the Great Lakes. At last count in 2020 there were sixty-four. Piping plovers are unusual among endangered species in that they have plenty of habitat—their only requirement for nesting seems to be beaches strewn with stones and pebbles. Unfortunately, they've taken a big hit during the past century because the places where they nest happen to be popular with people, and because as ground nesters their eggs and young are susceptible to predation by animals such as raccoons, gulls, and unleashed cats and dogs.

The day of our walk was rainy, with a strong warm wind blowing whitecaps on the lake. Craig and I forded the Platte River near the mouth. Most of the beach there is fenced off to keep people away from plover nesting sites. The nests themselves are protected by rectangular "exclosure" pens that keep predators out while allowing adult and fledgling plovers to come and go. We saw none of the birds that morning, but I told Craig about my friend Keith Taylor not long before watching a young boy throwing stones at plovers where we now stood. Keith approached the parents and as diplomatically as he could directed their attention to what their child was doing. They weren't pleased with Keith for interfering, and puffed up with indignation. "Why don't you mind your own—" they started to say, until Keith informed them that the fine for harassing an endangered species was $100,000 (which might or might not have been true). That got their attention.

Craig and I headed south along the beach, toward Point Betsie. Squalls raced parallel to us, obliterating the lake with diagonal sheets of rain. Waves came in lines of froth that broke over the offshore bar, gathered themselves, then attacked the beach.

The waves and wind made it necessary to shout to be heard, and we shouted all morning because there was much to talk about. Craig notices little things—a single white vertebra from a carp, the elegant meandering of swash lines, live crayfish and frogs struggling in the wash.

Now and then he looked up at the bigger view. He's a scientist with a philosopher's heart. Once he stopped and breathed deeply and said he'd forgotten how good the lake smells. "You ever notice," he asked, "the way big places overwhelm the senses until a sort of uber-sense takes over and you perceive all of it at once, gestalt-like?"

4.

Everybody grows immune to the wonders of the world, though our appreciation can be reignited. A friend once told me that she hosted a party of visitors from Japan who had never been to our part of the world and were so astonished by the immensity of Lake Michigan that at each stop of their tour—at the beach at Empire, at Otter Creek, at Point Betsie—they insisted on trooping to the shore and dipping their hands into the water and tasting it. They were amazed, every time, to find it was fresh.

Once your perceptions have been awakened, they rush at you. You notice that the beach changes character every mile or so. A stretch of clean sand, soothing to bare feet, is followed by a stretch of sole-bruising gravel. Next comes a cobble of stones sorted by size, pea-sized in the swash, fruit-sized farther up. Then sandy beach again, but now wide and sloping gently uphill to the back dunes. Around the next point it narrows, squeezed nearly to the water by tumbling hills of old dunes overgrown with birch, spruce, and leaning cedar. You can see the handiwork of the glaciers here.

Then there's a section of boulder gardens, the large rocks worn round, a few halved by ice, all thrown about in that randomness we find so aesthetically pleasing and which landscape architects and Japanese gardeners seek to replicate.

You might notice the colors of the rocks: pink, dull yellow, sullied white, black, slate-gray, middle-aged gray, rainy-day gray, rat-fur gray—dozens of shades of gray.

The waves vary, too, depending on the composition of the lake bottom. Lapping waves become turbulent around rocks. And more musical. You can hear the clatter of pebbles as the waves withdraw.

5.

At the Big Rock, artist Glenn Wolff and I dropped our daypacks, kicked off our sandals, and charged into the waves. The day was hot and windy, with three-foot rollers marching in ranks to the shore. Apparently we had the entire beach from Point Betsie to Frankfort to ourselves. It was a Wednesday. Ordinarily we'd be working. Today we knew the giddy freedom of kids playing hooky from school.

We swam for a while, then Glenn waded to shore. I stood waist-deep in the water with my back to the lake. It made me happy to notice that the waves running to the beach appeared to be rushing downhill. Now and then a large one would catch me by surprise from behind and body-slam me. That made me happy, too.

Glenn sat cross-legged on the Big Rock with his colored pencils and pad of paper and began to sketch. He sketched the cedars silhouetted at the top of the bluff above him. Then he turned and sketched the lake. That drawing now hangs on the wall of my office. It shows a distant boat on the horizon, with sunlight raining around it. In the foreground is a human bobbing in the water, about to be inundated by a breaker. The caption reads: "J.D. meets the perfect wave."

I waded from the water and stood beside Glenn, watching him work. I asked if there is a trick to capturing the essence of water.

"You have to define what's around it," he said.

I wasn't sure what he meant.

"Water is a problem of light and shadow," he said, "made more intricate by motion."

"Do you ever get it right?" I asked.

He grinned and said, "Never."

6.

Keith Taylor and I decided to see how much we could notice. He's a poet who recently retired from the University of Michigan, where he coordinated the undergraduate creative-writing program. He's also an accomplished birder and all-around terrific guy. He was staying for a few weeks in a rented house in Elberta, where he divided his time between translating a book of Greek poems and going outside to explore and watch birds.

We were curious to see the Grand Traverse Regional Land Conservancy's purchase at Green Point Dunes, south of Elberta, so we decided to walk that six-mile stretch to Arcadia. It is surely one of the most pristine freshwater beaches in the world, broad and clean, and backed by elaborate dunes blending into the forest. Saving it from development is one of the Conservancy's greatest achievements.

We were especially eager to see the enormous blow-out dune that aerial photos show as a deep U-shaped indentation off the beach between Green Point Dunes and the outlet of Lower Herring Lake. It might be the largest dune of its type in the Great Lakes.

Keith is a fine companion for many reasons, not least of which is his perpetually jolly demeanor and because he carries his knowledge lightly, while noticing everything. He spotted a merlin flying across the face of the bluff called Old Baldy—"exactly where you would expect to see it," he said, though I was looking elsewhere and missed it. It was the first merlin he had seen that year and brought his annual bird total for that year to 202 species. His life list is considerably longer.

Gulls stood in clusters on the dry sand, all facing into the wind. They begrudged having to make way as we approached. The nearest one turned a callous round eye on us, waited a moment longer in case we decided to leave, then bounced twice on its yellow stick legs and jumped into the air. It caught the wind and flared over the water. Then another went, and another, none of them in much of a hurry.

"Ringbill," said Keith. "See, they're smaller than the herrings. But where are the young ones? I haven't seen any of the young guys. They're the mottled gray ones you usually see."

A tern passed over the waves. Gulls are universally slandered as flying rats, but it's hard not to admire a tern for its sleek profile and graceful hinged wings. Gulls stand around like sullen smart-asses with too much time on their hands, but terns are all business. They hunt from the air, just offshore, where stunned shiners and alewives make easy pickings, soaring with their black-masked heads and rapier beaks bent ninety degrees down from their bodies. Then comes the sudden fold and dive and the jackknife plunge into the water. A second later they're back in the air, and you might glimpse a wriggling shard of silver as they turn a minnow in their beaks and swallow it. Instantly they're back on the hunt, heads down, eyes intent on the water again.

At some point Keith and I realized that we must have walked past the blow-out dune. We had been so busy talking that we missed a yawning mouth of sand a hundred yards wide leading into a blow-out bigger than a football stadium—so big that it shows up on satellite images from space. We laughed. The Great Observers. But it was a good excuse to come back another day.

Near Arcadia a string of houses are built on eroding bluffs close to the water. In an ongoing attempt to stabilize the bluffs from the ravages of high water the owners had dumped picnic-table-sized blocks of limestone over the banks and buried wooden groins in the lake bottom. Everything they had installed was being chewed away by the lake. We scrambled over the rocks and waded around the groins.

Ahead we could see the breakwall at Arcadia and the public beach crowded with people in bathing suits. Beyond was Manistee, Ludington, Grand Haven, a dozen cities culminating with Chicago, then the turn north into Wisconsin and eventually back to Michigan. Only one lake out of five, but a good start on those ten thousand miles.

When you think about it, there isn't much stopping a person from going all the way.

Creek Music

We had a weekend in a cabin on the Au Sable, and I couldn't wait to get in the water. Early the first morning I rigged my flyrod and waded into the riffle out front and had the river to myself for a while.

Then many happy people wearing swimsuits were floating past in inner tubes, all of them sunburned, with beer cans in hand, and asking in cheerful tones if I had caught anything. People across the river came down from the cottages, sat in lawn chairs, and they too asked if I had caught anything. "A few," I lied. The water was very low and clear, and I hadn't seen a single trout.

So I went exploring. And as often happens, I ended up exploring a small stream in a cedar swamp. This one was narrow enough to step over and quite fast, a prancing colt of a creek, tiny and high-spirited, in deep shadows dappled with only a few shafts of sunlight. It swerved around cedars and entered elbow-deep plunge pools bubbling with froth. The air was cool and carried the scent of cedar and moss, with a hint of decay.

Once I met a gentleman from Brooklyn who was visiting northern Michigan for the first time. He had flown from LaGuardia to Detroit, rented a car, and driven north on I-75. Over dinner he listened to my friends and me brag about this place—it's a weakness of ours and is one reason we make such dull companions—and finally he said, "What's the big deal? It's nothing but a bunch of trees."

I laughed. He was partly right, of course, but his view was too narrow. He could just as easily claim that Brooklyn is nothing but a bunch of brownstones.

Everyone knows that to begin to know a place you have to get out of your car and start walking. I would argue that you need to walk along the creeks and rivers. They're the secret alleys that lead behind billboards and storefronts to the back of a place, the side that is unadorned and without facade. Travelers on interstates have no idea it even exists. My grandfather, who was a farmer, would have snorted and said, "Claptrap! The only way to know the land is to work it." Maybe. Probably. But a creek can get you there too.

As can the trout in the creek. I've never forgotten the shock of holding my first trout in my hand. I was maybe eight years old, and already an experienced angler. We lived on Silver Lake then, where I was able to fish just about any time I wanted, casting off our dock or from neighbors' docks or from the shore itself. I had caught many northern pike and largemouth and smallmouth bass and panfish and a few walleye. I knew about trout, but they seemed as unlikely as unicorns. Fish with spots? Colors of the rainbow? But one day my father took me to a small, dark, cedar-shaded creek and showed me how to lower a worm into tiny pools and beneath cutbanks under the cedars, then left me to work it out for myself while he fished his own pools upstream.

I baited my hook with a wriggling garden worm and lowered into a frothy pool about the size of a bathroom sink. Immediately I felt an electric vibration of life and pulled a squirming, kicking fish from the water and swung it onto the bank, where I pinned it with my hands. And I've never been the same. To this day every trout I catch in a creek takes me back to childhood, when catching a brook trout was magical and transformative.

When my son Aaron was very young I took him to a tiny secret creek that flows through a swamp. At first he was tentative, not sure he wanted to get his shoes wet or his hands covered with worm goo. Then he caught his first trout, a rainbow maybe eight inches long, and it was like a light switched on. He turned feral before my eyes.

At one point, as we were sneaking up on the next little pool, Aaron froze in midstep. After a moment he turned to me and said in a whisper, "Listen. I hear music." We traced the sound to a tributary of the creek that was barely a foot wide. Not far upstream was a tiny waterfall pouring a rope of crystalline water into a gurgling pool. That was the source. That was the music he heard.

Boys of Summer

Ten was an age with some weight to it. Double digits. No more kid stuff, I figured. No more toys for Christmas. It struck me that I was likely to remain in double digits the rest of my life, unless science cured the deadly diseases. I couldn't shake the feeling that it was time to get a job and start saving for college.

The world my brother Rick and I knew was small then. It consisted of Long Lake, our house and yard, and a couple square miles of woods and meadows across the road. We sensed bigger places beyond, but lacked mobility.

The rowboat helped. Somehow Rick and I had convinced Dad to let us take it for the day. We'd been using it for years, but only with oars, and always within sight of the house. Now we wanted to borrow the little Johnson outboard our father had owned since before we were born. It was a temperamental motor, difficult to start and tricky to keep running, but I was confident we could handle it. After all, I had watched Dad take the carburetor apart many times, gently removing the speed needles and valve assembly and bathing them in a jar lid of gasoline, blowing them dry as if he were blowing on the breast feather of a swan, then carefully reassembling the parts, pumping the primer, and giving the starter cord a two-handed yank.

That morning we got up at dawn, while the lake was still calm. It would remain that way all day, a rare event. Usually by midmorning a breeze would come up and grow stronger as the afternoon progressed. But this day the lake stayed mirror calm.

Rick and I loaded the boat with our life jackets, a bag of sandwiches, a canteen of water, our masks, snorkels, and fins and a jug of extra gas. Our plan was to motor to the far end of the lake, four miles away, and dive for lost fishing lures and golf balls in the bays and around the islands. We had been there before, with our parents, but it always seemed like foreign territory. The kids at that end of the lake went to a different school and might as well have spoken a different language.

We made our way down the lake, the little engine chugging its reliable, one-stroke putter, until we reached the southernmost bay. That was where Long Lake exited through a narrow brushy creek. If we had been determined enough we could have dragged the boat down the creek to Mud Lake, then down the creek below it to Lake Ann, and from there descend the Platte River to Lake Michigan, then to Huron, Erie, Ontario, and the St. Lawrence, to the Atlantic and all the oceans on the planet. Our little world was growing bigger by the moment. All we had to do was go.

But I got careless and steered too close to shore and the propeller hit a rock and sheared a pin. I lifted the motor and tried to remove the propeller but I fumbled it and it fell into the water. We looked and looked, but couldn't find it.

So we rowed home. Rowed until our hands blistered, but we didn't care. We were on our own, under our own power and intoxicated with independence, rowing stroke after stroke into the future.

A Spur of the Moment Kind of Day

A few of us were sitting on a patio drinking beer and talking about good days—what makes them and why we value them and how you might not recognize one until it sneaks up and surprises you. You might not even realize you had a good day until much later.

It reminded me of a summer morning when my friend James McCullough stopped by unexpectedly. Strapped to the top of his truck was his notoriously heavy fiberglass canoe, "The Green Meany." It weighs so much that James and Tim Tibeau still talk about the agonies they suffered ten years ago while portaging it between lakes in Lake Superior Provincial Park. I already had plans for the day, but James was insistent, so I grabbed my fishing gear and jumped into his truck.

We drove to the north end of a lake we'd fished together a few times in the past. It's a narrow, shallow arm of a much larger lake renowned for its clear water and sand bottom. The shallow arm is much different. It has a silt bottom, and is encircled by lily pads and reeds. James announced that he would paddle while I fished, so I took the bow seat and rigged my rod and tied on a fake frog made from deer hair. For the next few hours James paddled us along the shore while I caught and released many largemouth and smallmouth bass up to three pounds. The fish were hiding in the vegetation, where they could ambush prey as it wandered past. I cast the frog and made it run over the top of the lily pads as if it was desperate to escape, and the bass below went bonkers and tried to kill it. It was a bluebird day in early June, warm and nearly windless. Just about perfect.

But in the afternoon the day made one of those 180-degree turns so common in Great Lakes country. First we noticed a few streamers of fog wraithing through the woods. Then a wind off Lake Michigan swept across the water and slammed into us. The temperature dropped twenty degrees in a few seconds, and suddenly we were shivering in our shorts and T-shirts. The wind grew stronger, waves grew into whitecaps, and it was time to put my rod away and take up one of James's big beavertail paddles. We set off paddling as hard as we could downwind toward the boat launch.

I doubt if the Green Meany has ever gone faster. We paddled in unison, reaching deep and pulling hard, until we were going so fast we overran the waves and were keeping pace with the banners of spray streaming from the wave tops.

Ahead of us was an aluminum fishing boat stalled in the water with two guys tinkering over the engine. Like us, they were probably locals. On a lake ringed by multimillion-dollar "cottages" owned by downstaters, they were the guys the owners called when their furnace quit, or the plumbing was acting up, or they needed a cord of firewood delivered before a dinner party. As James and I came abreast of them they gave up on the outboard and engaged their electric trolling motor and steered silently downwind not quite as fast as we were going.

James said to me, "I've seen those guys before. They catch a lot of walleye." He raised his voice and asked if they remembered meeting him last winter ice fishing on Burt Lake. "You know," he called, "that day you caught so many walleyes."

The older of the two men looked puzzled and called back, "Was it in front of the Happy Hour?"

"That must be the place," James answered. "Was it you who caught so many that day?"

The guy said, "Yeah, we did okay, but I don't remember you," and James laughed and said "That's because I wasn't there." The guy looked even more puzzled, until his younger companion, maybe his son, laughed and said "You been had." Because, of course, now James knew a good place to fish for walleyes on Burt Lake.

And all of us were laughing. We laughed because of the good-hearted exchange across the water. Because of the fish we had caught that day and the fish that James would probably catch next winter. Because of the fog that had filtered through the trees from Lake Michigan and the sudden cold and wind that followed. Because we were flying downwind surrounded by whitecaps in an absurdly heavy canoe we liked more with every stroke of our paddles.

That was a good day.

Surprised by Beauty

In September my son Aaron and I helped deliver a 64-foot sloop from Charlevoix to Toronto. We packed foul-weather gear and a change of clothes and Aaron's cameras—he's a documentary filmmaker—and joined a crew of four others and set off before daylight from the marina on Round Lake, under the city lights of Charlevoix.

We motored beneath the lift bridge on Bridge Street and down the Pine River canal into Lake Michigan. Then we raised the sails to catch a snapping wind and were on our way.

Years from now I'll remember the Straits, with the Mackinac Bridge off our bow, where Aaron filmed the crew discussing why the aged Line 5 petroleum pipeline should be removed from the bottom of the Straits before it ruptures catastrophically. The owner of the boat, a businessman from Detroit, argued for the economic necessities of clean water and air. The rest of us outlined ethical, aesthetic, and commonsense arguments.

I'll remember sailing through the night on lakes Huron and Erie, watching the glow of cities on the horizon and freighters lit as brightly as stadiums. The late hours on Lake Erie are especially vivid, when Aaron and I sat with Captain Geoff at the helm telling stories beneath stars so bright I thought we would bump them with our masts.

I'll remember passing through the locks at the Welland Canal, those engineering marvels whose history is entwined with the upper lakes and the entire continent beyond, and the storm on Lake Ontario, when a line of squalls overran us with fifty-mile-an-hour winds that raised waves to eight feet in a heartbeat and tore the bimini cover from the cockpit. Black clouds swept down from the north and the air temperature dropped twenty degrees in ten minutes.

But the best moment was at the end of the second day, when we were sailing down the Detroit River at sunset. It was a gorgeous evening, the summer's best, and people were outside enjoying it. Pleasure craft of every description were on the river, from canoes and kayaks to fishing boats and yachts. On shore pedestrians walked in pairs along the Riverwalk. Anglers—solitary or in small groups—sat on lawn chairs with their rods leaning against the railings.

As the sun neared the horizon, it suddenly bathed the world in light and color. It was what photographers call the "magic hour," when sunlight passes through the long breadth of the atmosphere, as if through a thousand miles of sheer silk. It washed everything around us in showers of scarlet and gold. Sunlight streamed in rays through the city, between skyscrapers and apartment buildings, past the Renaissance Center and Cobo and Joe Louis Arena. Then the light sprawled across the river like a golden quilt and climbed the brick buildings along the Windsor waterfront.

It was stunning and mesmerizing and it gave me much to think about. Sometimes this up-north guy needs to be reminded that the Detroit waterfront is one of the finest places in Michigan.

In the Upper Country

Lately when I look into Lake Superior I can see the centuries passing. It must be the clarity of the water. Observers three and four centuries ago remarked, as we do today, on the brightly colored stones thirty feet below, the water so cold and crystalline it's like looking up at the stars at night. When we see the same water and sky that the earliest people saw, the sweep of history carries us along.

Limnologists tell us that Lake Superior is oligotrophic—a young lake. All five Great Lakes remain geological adolescents, but we who live among them have grown older. In 1535, when Jacques Cartier ascended the St. Lawrence River to what is now Montreal and learned there were vast seas to the west, Leonardo da Vinci had been dead only sixteen years and Copernicus was demonstrating mathematically the heretical assertion (and burnable offense) that the earth orbited the sun and not vice versa. By the time a sickly band of Separatists from the Church of England landed at Plymouth in 1620, the French explorer Étienne Brûlé had already spent ten years exploring the Great Lakes and their surrounding forests, the land then known as *le pays d'en haut*, the Upper Country.

Of course the place has changed much since then. A fine recent book by environmental historian Nancy Langston, *Sustaining Lake Supe-*

rior, documents the changes of the past as well as those we're likely to see in the future. Among the most significant of them, and one you've noticed if you've spent much time on Lake Superior, is that it is warming. Researchers say the average surface temperature has increased 4.5 degrees Fahrenheit since 1979, enough, writes Langston, to explain why algae blooms are showing up where they had never been seen and why invasive species are expanding their ranges. Another consequence of the general warming is that snowfall amounts are declining and major rain events are increasing, causing contaminants from municipal wastewater systems and farmland to wash into the lake. Additionally, surrounding forests will likely become stressed, resulting in dieoffs that trigger wildfires, erosion, and runoff of sediment and debris into Superior and its tributaries.

Luckily, not all the changes are so ominous. People are more committed to protecting the lake than they were fifty or a hundred years ago, and their children might prove to be even more so. We've also learned that ecosystems, with their interconnected populations of plants and animals, have an impact that extends hundreds or thousands of miles, making it everyone's business to protect, conserve, and restore them. And, best of all, Lake Superior country remains the wildest and most majestic place in the middle of the continent. It's no wonder we're so passionate about defending it.

Historians say that on much of Superior there is less boat traffic now than at any time since the age of the fur traders. Travelers from the late 18th to the early 20th centuries wrote often about how busy the lake was. Every day and sometimes every hour they met Ojibwa or French-Canadian voyageurs in canoes, barges rowed by British soldiers, schooners with their decks piled high with lumber or their holds heavy with copper, or chugging steamers carrying immigrants, tourists, and cargo.

Yet, when you travel by boat today you can't help notice that a few miles past the cities and their safe harbors you have the lake mostly to yourself. A distant ore carrier might break the horizon, and jet trails will probably trace the sky. Otherwise it's just you, the water, and the sky, as it has been since the beginning.

Making Trail

When we were boys, about eight and ten years old, my brother and I built a trail through the woods. The woods were across the road from our house on Long Lake—a couple hundred acres of second- or third-growth beech, maple, and hemlock on rolling hills that covered much of the peninsula between Long Lake and Mickey Lake. Deep in the woods, at the bottom of a winding moss-covered trail beneath the hemlocks, was Bullhead Lake, a small woodland pond ringed with lily pads and drowned timber that we visited regularly to search for frogs and turtles and occasionally to fish. It wasn't very deep, so whenever there was a winter with too much ice and snow for sunlight to penetrate, all the fish would die of winter-kill. For a year or two afterwards, our bobbers would float immobile on the surface when we fished. Then, mysteriously, a summer would come when the bobbers would tremble and we would pull in bluegills a few inches long and now and then a bass as long as our hands. The next year they would be keepers. The year after that they would die off again.

Rick and I wanted a shortcut to the house of our friends, the Houghton boys. They lived two miles away by paved road, half that distance if we cut through the woods. It would be quicker if we could ride our bikes the whole way, but we had to walk our bikes through the woods, slowing us intolerably. So one summer Rick and I decided to do something about it.

We built it from scratch and, like most trails, it meandered. We wanted it to be the shortest route possible, but fallen trees and old stumps kept getting in our way, so we applied some geographical logic and followed the natural contours and corridors of the land.

It was hard work. We dragged small fallen trees and branches out of the way and raked many years' worth of decaying leaves aside. Inch by inch we stomped the newly exposed ground until we packed it hard enough to support our bikes. I don't remember how long it took us—maybe a couple weeks, maybe most of the summer—but finally we had carved our shortcut through the woods. In no time at all it was as if it had been there forever. It remains there to this day.

We rode it almost daily on our one-speed bikes with their semi-fat tires and of course we always went as fast as we could. Down the trail, legs pumping, hurtling past trees and hanging branches, banking around curves, gaining speed on the downhills until we were sure we would launch into flight. We'd hit the gravel two-track skidding, bank right, and stand on our pedals and pump furiously to climb the small incline where a great horned owl once chased me with a warning swoop so close to the back of my head that I could feel the air displaced by its wings. Then we raced through the red-pine plantation, reached the shoulder of North Long Lake Road, coasted down one hill and pedaled up another, and arrived at our friends' house. More often than not, all of us would return to the lake and go swimming. The shortcut shaved off ten or fifteen minutes every trip. More importantly, it taught us that though we were just kids we could get things done. We were self-reliant. We could stay on a job until it was finished. We could make a mark on the world.

The trail is used now more than ever. You can walk it yourself. It's the well-marked route into the Bullhead Lake Natural Area, a Michigan Natural Resources Trust Fund site that was purchased and saved from development by a group of volunteers led by our former neighbor Annie Gurian. The trail is worn so deep now it looks as if it were made centuries ago, and I'm sure many people assume it's no different than countless other old trails in Michigan that lead to interesting and out-of-the-way places.

But this one was built by children.

August Explorations

Somehow August never quite lives up to its promise. In winter, we look ahead to it as the lazy middle of summer, when every day is so long that there's plenty of time to go biking or boating in the morning, meet friends for lunch, then work in the garden all afternoon. In the evening you can grill something for dinner, then listen to the Tigers on the radio while watching fireflies blinking in the yard. And that's just one day.

But then August arrives and the days fling past as quickly as they do in every other month. What were we thinking? August isn't deep summer— it's the beginning of autumn. The days are growing shorter, splashes of red are showing in the maples, and at night there's a bite of cold in the air. The machinery of the seasons is clanking along, as always, and suddenly we realize that we have to get outside *now* to go fishing, hiking, boating, golfing—whatever it is we love to do in summer.

Those of us whose preferences tend to involve water are lucky to live in Michigan, where there are more creeks, rivers, lakes, ponds, and Great Lakes shorelines than anyone could explore in a lifetime. August might not be the best time to fish the inland lakes—the water is at its warmest then and most of the fish have gone deep—but it's the best month for poking around in places beyond your usual tramping grounds. The weather is usually dry, so dirt roads and two-tracks are in good shape, and mosquitoes are past their peak, making it a fine time to bushwhack through cedar swamps in search of creeks and beaver ponds. Also it's blueberry season, so even when the fishing isn't great, the foraging can be. Blueberries are one of the bonuses of the season.

An even bigger bonus is the knowledge that accumulates with the seasons and the years. Explore a place long enough and it becomes part of your life. Its history merges with your history and pretty soon it's impossible to separate the two. It's a lifetime effort. You can go at it methodically, planning expeditions across the state, studying maps and guidebooks, interviewing local experts, initiating conversations with strangers at the supermarket. Or you can let it happen at its own pace, organically, until the day you look around and realize you've found your favorite place.

One of my own favorites is located—well, never mind where it's located. What matters is that we find our own favorites. And it pays to stay alert while you're doing it. The world is full of surprise gifts. Those wild blueberries are one that you can carry home and share with your family and friends. If it's a fruitful year, seal a quart or two in bags and hide them in the back of the freezer. They'll be delicious come February.

Making Memories

A friend was telling me about a rustic lakefront cabin that two generations of his family have rented every summer since 1950. That struck
me as a fine tradition, so I asked what he liked best about it. Without
hesitation he said, "Making memories."

Many of us have found that cottages, cabins, and camps are ver-
itable memory incubators. Their walls are practically drenched with
them. Funny how it works, though. The memories that rise to prom-
inence as the years pass might not be the ones you expect. Not the
Fourth of July celebration watching fireworks, but running around the
yard catching fireflies. Not learning to water-ski behind a powerboat,
but rowing to the island in a leaky wooden rowboat. It's like taking a
toddler to the zoo. You lead her to the elephant enclosure expecting
her to be astonished, but all she wants to look at are the sparrows hopping around at her feet.

One bright memory that comes back to me often is sitting in
lounge chairs with our friends Jim and Mary Ann in front of their
cabin on Platte Lake. It was a warm, humid July night and we were
enjoying that feeling of contentment that comes at the end of a long
day spent in the sun, in boats, swimming, fishing, playing lawn games,
cooking over a grill.

As we chatted and poked the bonfire, we became aware of flashes of lightning low in the sky across the lake. "Heat lightning" we used to call it when we were kids, though meteorologists assure us there's no such thing: it's regular lightning so far away that the sound of the thunder can't reach us. It occurs often on summer nights simply because that's when masses of warm humid air are most likely to rise and meet cool air—the basic conditions for thunder and lightning.

The lightning that night was flashing silently inside mountainous, anvil-topped thunderheads towering above the horizon north of us. Someone was getting pounded by a storm. We tried to guess how far away it might be. Thirty miles? Fifty? Jim pulled out his phone and checked the radar map, and we were astonished to see that the only thunderstorm in the upper Great Lakes region sat squarely on top of the Straits of Mackinac, 130 miles from us.

Earlier that evening, just before dark, we had sat in our chairs watching the kids while they fished from the end of the dock. They were casting bobbers and worms and had caught a few small perch. I was surprised they caught anything at all. The water there is shallow and lacks cover; not a place that should attract fish. But suddenly Chris had reared back on his rod, bending it double, and a largemouth bass that must have weighed four pounds leaped from the water, ran for the drop-off, and promptly broke the line. I checked Chris's reel and discovered the drag had malfunctioned, but no matter. It was the biggest fish anyone could remember being hooked from the dock—maybe the biggest fish they had seen hooked in the lake, period—and you can be sure Chris will never forget it.

Summer Work and High Water

Lately everyone I know is talking about the record high water in the Great Lakes. It's a subject of particular urgency to waterfront dwellers, some of whom have had the misfortune of watching their homes tumble into the lakes. Is it a consequence of climate change? Or a natural cycle?

Both, it seems. There's no doubt that the warming planet is having an impact on the Great Lakes. Temperatures are warming decade by decade, and annual precipitation is increasing—up ten percent since 1901, according to a recent study. Even more significantly, the frequency of major storm events is increasing. As a result, water levels rise and fall more dramatically than they used to.

They've always risen and fallen, of course. In the early 1970s Lakes Michigan and Huron were nearly as high as they are now. Bluffs collapsed, houses slid into the waves, entire beaches disappeared. In Chicago a storm surge shoved yachts across Lake Shore Drive and stranded them on the median. Property owners searched desperately for ways to protect their homes.

At the end of my junior year of high school I answered an ad for what sounded like the perfect summer job. It was placed by a University of Michigan student named Stan who had an idea for slowing beach erosion and needed manual laborers. It was outside work, on the beach near Empire. What could be better? He hired me, but with misgivings. "You're kinda skinny," he said.

Stan's plan was to build wooden breakwalls that would jut into Lake Michigan and interrupt the longshore current that sweeps north up the coast. His theory was that when the current strikes a breakwall it slows enough to drop its load of suspended sand in front of the structure and stabilizes the beach.

The theory was sound, but it had a flaw. It turned out that much of the sand that collected at each breakwall, or "groin" as such structures are sometimes called, was stolen from the beach immediately beyond it. Stan didn't consider that a problem. In fact, it was a bonus. Every time we erected a breakwall, the owner of the adjacent property needed one too.

We built the structures with rough-sawn poplar planks sixteen feet long and two inches thick that we hauled from a truck in the public parking lot down to the beach. We laid the planks atop long cedar pilings on the sand and nailed them together with 20-penny nails. The assembled structures were so heavy that it required four of us to drag them into the water. We would float them into position perpendicular to the beach and heft them upright on their piling legs. Then we struggled to hold them steady against the onslaught of waves while Stan fired up his gas-powered water-jet, powered by a pump with a gasoline engine which sat on the beach and was equipped with a short intake hose for sucking water from the lake and a longer hose for firing it back out. He would jam the nozzle underwater against the foot of each piling and blow the sand and gravel away in a furious, tumultuous churn. Gradually the weight of the structure would settle the pilings five or six feet into the lake bottom, until the lowest plank rested on the bottom and the upper ones stood above the surface of the water.

When the work went well we could install two or three breakwalls in a day. But the work rarely went well. Waves broke over the tops of our chest waders and sometimes wrenched the walls from our hands and knocked them over. We frequently encountered rocks too large for the jet to dislodge and would have to shatter them or pry them aside with steel bars and sledgehammers. It was some of the hardest work I've ever done.

By the end of the summer we had installed twenty or thirty breakwalls along a half-mile of shore. They stuck out from the shore like a row of suburban fences, and the sand they collected gave the beach a scalloped appearance that we were certain would halt any further erosion. The property owners were pleased, and Stan had made a hefty profit. He asked if I wanted to come back and work for him the next summer. I said I didn't think so.

All that winter, every time the wind came up, I imagined waves and icebergs slamming against the breakwalls. In April I drove to the shore in Empire to see how they'd held up.

Gone. Not a trace.

Autumn

The Fringe of Autumn

Every year there's a day when summer gives way to autumn. Last year it began before dawn on September 30, when a powerful wind shifted from the southwest to the northwest and funneled down the Great Lakes and the temperature fell from the 50s to near 40. By midmorning, waves had reached ten and twelve feet. NOAA measured one rogue near the center of Lake Michigan at twenty feet.

A week earlier Gail and I had walked to the meadow behind our house and found summer still lingering. It was September 23, the autumn equinox, but except for the brilliant scarlet of the sumac it could have been July. We walked through goldenrod, knapweed, thistle, and New England aster, all in robust blossom. Honeybees droned and grasshoppers skittered ahead of us.

Usually we've had a spell of cold weather by the end of September, but last year the season was slow to change. There had been no frost and none of those sudden, slanting rains so characteristic of autumn in Great Lakes country. The days stayed bright and warm and the nights mild.

Of course we knew all the things we love about fall were coming, followed, perhaps sooner than we wished, by winter. We'd begun noticing subtle changes in August, when the afternoon light grew brassy as the sun eased lower, and the nights began to cool. Starlings were flocking and lining up on telephone lines, sometimes in such numbers that the wires sagged dangerously. Along the Great Lakes shores monarch butterflies fluttered southward on their staggered migration that would end, generations later, in the mountains of Mexico. People on the beach lay in the sun or swam, but you could sense an urgency. They knew every day might be the last.

Autumn reminds us to enjoy such days. It reminds us, also, of transience and mortality. I mentioned once to Emily Thompson, who is a biologist at Washtenaw Community College, that I sensed oblivion in the air when apples started falling to the ground to rot and animals disappeared into their burrows for the winter. Emily pointed out that I was being short-sighted. The seeds in decaying fruit and the animals that hibernate are not falling into oblivion, she insisted, but merely waiting for spring. They are "sort of spring-loaded," she said, "ready to bust out with offspring at the first warm weather."

We're spring-loaded, too, and can take comfort knowing that renewal is waiting on the other side of the sun. In the meantime we have October, the scent of burning leaves, hunting camp, the flame-like colors in the trees, those slanting rains rattling against the window. That morning last year when waves rushed the length of Lake Michigan and the temperature plummeted, I slipped into a down jacket, put on a wool cap, and walked out to meet the season.

The Many Autumns

When I was a kid I liked fall best, October especially, month of my birth, of crisp nights and colored leaves, of Halloween and apple cider and firewood that had to be split and stacked before winter. Summer was trivial, made for children and tourists, but autumn was somber, solemn, mature. It made me impatient to grow up. On windy October and November days when I was twelve years old I would stand on the shore of Long Lake and watch the year get swept away and be overwhelmed with a delicious sorrow. The season clarified me. It was sepulchral. It was elegiac. I savored its bittersweet tang.

The poet Donald Hall once wrote that Michigan's fall is like Europe's—"burnished old gold; yellow harvest mellow with violins; Autumn of the falling fruit and the long journey toward oblivion; muted and melancholy . . ."—though surely he was thinking of Ann Arbor, where he once lived and taught, and not the wooded and hilly rural north, where autumn's colors boom in operatic excess. Up here is as different from Ann Arbor as Eagle Pond is from Cambridge. But Hall was right about the melancholy, the falling fruit, and the journey toward oblivion. We have all three in abundance. Every dropped leaf, every skidding rain, every flock of geese passing overhead reminds us of winter's approach. Were the days a movie, the soundtrack would be mostly cellos. We become suddenly industrious and hurry outside to gather all the music and fragrance we can hold, stocking up on sensations for the sterile months ahead. If we must stay indoors we put on a kettle of water for tea, settle into a chair beside the fireplace, and open the first of the season's thick novels. Either way, we're digging in against oblivion.

By the calendar, fall begins on the autumnal equinox, September 23, and ends on the winter solstice, December 22, though everyone in the upper latitudes knows it extends from the first yellow leaves to the first enduring snowfall. Here in northern Michigan, that means from the middle of September to the middle of November most years, though the earliest intimations come in August, when we notice that the sun has been slipping a little farther southward every day and is starting to give off a burnished and more contrasty light. Late in August comes the first cold night, maybe some frost in the lowlands, and suddenly it's fruit-fly season. In the afternoons the sky is clear and very blue—summer's haze has drifted away—and at night the stars are brilliant. Even the mornings have an afternoon feel.

A couple weeks into September the nights turn cold and frost blackens the tops of the tomato plants. In the morning if we forget to put on a jacket before stepping outside, we hurry back inside to grab one. The change alerts us. It makes us want to lift a corner of the world to see what's hiding beneath.

Then comes October, full autumn, when we look back at September as late summer, and ahead to November as early winter. All the things I like best in fall—crisp air and grouse and woodcock and spawning brook trout and maple leaves spiraling to the ground and autumn colors reflected off still water on a lake—peak in October. It never comes now without rekindling a memory from October 1, 1996, when Tom Carney and I were driving near Frederick, on our way to Tom's cabin on the Thunder Bay River, and pulled over to the side of the road to watch two bull elk sparring in a field. They faced off against each other, lowered their heads, and touched their broad antlers as if they were fencers about to begin a match. And then they got down to business.

October gives us Indian Summer, that oddly named respite, the return for a few days or a week of summer breeze scented with apples and burning leaves, when the sky and Lake Michigan are the same intense blue, and the woods are flaming with reds and oranges. It's also harvest time—crates heaped with apples and pears, pumpkins on the porch, freezers filled with bounty—and we have to hurry to get chores finished before the cold returns. Because the warm days will be gone soon, we're reluctant to enjoy them. It's a skepticism typical of those who live with extremes of weather. We can never quite trust a kindness.

Then comes descending fall, the namesake season, when leaves drop and bitter rain slants from a sky that a few minutes ago was empty and blue. Fall. The word has finality in it. A gust, another rattling of rain, and leaves plummet, landing with a slap on the windshield. These cold autumn rains are always the same: frequent, wind-flurried, and in five minutes they're over.

Deep autumn follows, when frost covers every surface in the morning and the afternoons turn radiant. It's the season of autumn songs: geese high overhead, the surf-like rhythms of wind in the treetops, a chainsaw rising to a wail in the distance. The colors of the land are muted now to earthy browns and grays, and the orange coats of hunters are the brightest objects you're likely to see. Yellow leaves lay plastered on the road, like handprints painted in the night as a warning or a benediction. In the woods the trees are mostly bare now. The air is scented with a rich decay.

In late fall the north wind makes the doors and windows bang: Macbeth's wind, time's knock, the winds of mortality. The days grow short. Chickadees hunker in the shrubbery, resting between dashes to the feeder. Sleet turns to pellets of snow that bounce across the frozen gravel in the driveway, while the cold sucks the water from puddles, leaving them empty and paned with ice. It's the time of storms on the Great Lakes, when the temperature can drop thirty degrees in an hour and gales push waves fifteen feet high where a few hours ago the surface was calm. Small boats are dry-docked for the winter, but the giant tankers and ore carriers risk a final run before ice closes the lakes.

Finally it's last-of-fall, the end of the season, when autumn merges with winter. This is mostly an indoor time for those of us who don't hunt whitetails or work outside, so I look for reasons to go out. There was an afternoon years ago, around Thanksgiving, when my oldest son and I drove to the park at Bowers Harbor to play basketball on what would be our final outing of the year. Aaron was fourteen then, that most awkward of ages for boys, when they are no longer children and not yet men. He wore the same size shoes as I and was nearly as tall, but he was still growing into his size and needed to test himself against his father. Every day we shot baskets at the park or threw a football around in our yard or wrestled in the living room or locked wrists over the dining room table. Aaron hooted whenever he triumphed. It was all in fun, but beneath every contest ran a current of solemnity.

It was cold that afternoon at Bowers Harbor, not much above freezing, and the wind was from the north, sharp and gusting, carrying the scent of snow. I remember the sky was a streaming flood of dark clouds that turned the day to gloom an hour before sunset. We had the asphalt court to ourselves, and played one-on-one, make it and take it, schoolyard rules. Soon perspiration soaked through our sweatshirts, but we did not stop to rest because we knew we would grow chilled if we did. It was possible to be too cold and too warm at the same moment. I licked my lips and tasted the ocean.

The sky grew darker as the day slid toward its end, and finally I held the ball and suggested we go home and get showers and dinner. Aaron laughed. It was a joke between us—the Old Guy wants to quit before he loses. The score was 10–6, Aaron's lead. First to eleven would win.

"My ball," he said, and I checked it to him.

And at that moment, as Aaron caught the ball against his chest, the clouds parted low on the horizon and the sun escaped through the crack and sprayed the world with light. Everything around us was suddenly vivid with brilliant reds and radiant golds. The vineyard beyond the park, the bare maples along the road, Aaron's bright face and blue eyes and the orange basketball in his hands—everywhere I looked, every tangible thing had become magnificent. I was stunned. After many days of gray clouds and rain, we had been presented with a gift of color.

"Look!" cried Aaron, pointing toward the wind-streaked water of West Bay and the hills of Leelanau beyond it, and my heart soared because of course I want my sons to discover beauty and grace in the world and for their lives to be enriched beyond measure—and when I turned in the direction he pointed, he drove past me to the basket for an easy layup.

"Eleven-six," he said. "My game."

His game, his day. And soon enough—perhaps in another bittersweet season of downturn and decay, of whispers, vespers, and evensong—his world.

A Riot of Colors, with Violins

Gail and I were paddling our canoe across a small lake in October, when my vocabulary failed me. To employ a weary cliché, the woods surrounding the lake were ablaze in a "riot" of autumn colors. I lifted a brown leaf from the water, held it up, and asked Gail what color she saw. "Burnt sienna," she said. For a moment I was perplexed. Then I remembered the crayons of childhood. And something I read once that mentioned the red earth mined from Siena, Italy. How much of the world does an oak leaf contain? Plenty, it seems.

I'm lucky that so many of my family and friends are artists, for now and then they allow me to see the world through their eyes. My own view might be as drab as burlap, but they see Day-Glo swirls of texture and shadow. When they talk about light and color I try not to miss a word.

Over dinner not long ago the conversation turned to the color palette of a place. It was a new idea for me: That every place on earth has a visual fingerprint derived from the colors of its unique combination of plants, soil, buildings, lakes, rivers, sky—even the "gray and buff" of its underlying, unseen bedrock, according to one of the more cryptically minded friends at the table. That same friend described how she once color-chipped the trees in her yard to determine the colors she wanted to paint her outdoor furniture. Another insisted that in sum-

mer the reflections off Lake Michigan filter through the pines in Glen
Arbor and saturate the village with a shade of blue found no place else.
That led somehow to a discussion of the rhythms of the seasons and
how we're hardwired to adjust our circadian cadences to match them.
That in turn led to someone recalling a recent discovery by physicists
that a kind of tuning fork vibrates in the nucleus of every atom in the
universe—and that it vibrates at the same frequency as the bass string
of a violin. A musician among us said it was scientific validation of the
ancient claim that composers and performers tap into nothing less
than the music of the spheres.

I was thinking of those conversations the day Gail and I crossed
the lake. When we reached shore we pulled our canoe up on the
sand and took a walk around the shore. When we reached the far
side we looked back and admired the colors of the woods and their
reflections on the water. It was a riot of yellows, oranges, reds, and
greens. An uproar of autumn colors. A tumult, a melee, a brawl. I'm
still looking for a better phrase.

Once, on Isle Royale, a young man chastised me for bringing a red
canoe into a wilderness area. It was summer, and everything around
us was mostly blue or green. "I could see your canoe all the way across
the bay," the young man said, his voice trembling with outrage. "It's an
eyesore. It's color pollution."

But in October our boat could offend no one. I see it now: a splash
of scarlet in a brilliant world, with violins playing in the background.
That day our beautiful canoe fit right in. And, for once, so did we.

The Autumn Trail

When I need to be alone I often hike a trail that follows a wooded ridge above Lake Michigan. Usually I go with some purpose in mind. Maybe it's for exercise, which I can surely use. Or to hunt for mushrooms, or to harvest wild leeks, or to see if the autumn warblers are passing through on their way south. Maybe it's just an urge to discover something new. What, after all, is more basic to being human? We've always been compelled to see what's on the other side of a hill or around the next bend; to follow roads, trails, and creeks; to uncover what is hidden. It has driven us from valley to valley, from continent to continent, and will presumably drive us, in some distant or maybe not-so-distant future, from planet to planet.

Many have argued that the best reason to set out in search of discoveries—to walk a trail, to get outdoors in general—is for the physical and psychological benefits. Studies demonstrate empirically what most of us probably know intuitively: getting outside is good for us. It lowers our blood pressure, clears our minds, enhances our sense of well-being. Regularly stepping away from the ruckus of ordinary life might be the best prescription for good health.

But if we're honest with ourselves we have to admit that being purposeful all the time can become tiresome. Every moment doesn't have to be devoted to self-improvement. We're even allowed to waste a little time. I think of the words of an ancient Chinese poet describing an excursion to the country: "I went and returned. It was nothing special."

Nothing special might be just what the doctor ordered. The pressure's off. For once you don't have to check off any items on your to-do list. Just let the hours unspool. Let the miles unspool, too. In the process, somehow, without making a big deal about it, you settle into your true self. Whatever that is. Let's say your unworried self, the one without ambition or anxiety. It's just you on the trail with your thoughts.

It's funny, though, how often it happens that when we abandon our expectations we stumble across something quite wonderful. No doubt it's because we notice more than we realize. Our perceptions sneak up on us and slip notes into our pockets that we later discover and read. It's as if the world can tap us on the shoulder to see if we're paying attention. Most of the time, of course, we're not. And that's fine, too.

Those very thoughts were on my mind not long ago as I walked the Ridge Trail. I had just stopped at the overlook, the one spot on the trail with an unobstructed view of East Bay, and was thinking about perception and attention, and probably about work, money, mortality, or some other foolishness, and was startled and offended—this was not my intention at all!—when hundreds of starlings burst from the trees around me. The rush of their wings as they took flight sounded like a sudden shower of rain. Somehow I had never noticed that before.

A Round River

Glenn Wolff and I got lost on the Crystal River. That isn't easy to do. The Crystal, in Leelanau County, is one of Michigan's prettiest rivers but it flows only six miles from Big Glen Lake to Lake Michigan. It's an even shorter distance as the crow flies, but a crow flies straight and the Crystal is anything but. It meanders in long, exaggerated sweeps that on a map look like they were made by a seismograph during a major tremor.

It was mid-September of a drought year when Glenn and I waded a section of the Crystal to fish for bass and pike. The day was so hot that it seemed more like the middle of the summer than the beginning of fall. We brought sandwiches, but only one small bottle of drinking water. Our plan was to wade from the cofferdam to the first bridge, then walk the road back to the car.

This was a way of fishing that my father and his brother-in-law, my Uncle Jim, enjoyed on the Crystal in the early 1950s, when my father was fresh out of the Army and was in love with Jim's sister. He and Jim would wade downstream and cast plugs and live bait into the deep holes and catch fish much bigger than you would expect from such a small river. I've seen the pictures. Nice fish, held proudly by young men with dazzling smiles.

Below the cofferdam Glenn and I spotted a northern pike at the edge of the plunge pool, but it refused to strike. Our flies were more harassment than enticement, and finally the fish became annoyed and swam away downstream.

We continued on, wading through the shallows and fishing the small pools at the bends and beneath overhanging cedars, any place that might hold a fish. Much of the bottom of the Crystal is sand, interspersed with stretches of gravel, with mother-of-pearl glittering in the sun. A few early Chinook had built redds in the riffles. We watched the aggressive males chasing rivals and creating havoc, their broad backs out of the shallow water, slicing vees in the surface. While the boys cavorted, the females took over the redds, turned on their sides, and beat the gravel clean with powerful thrusts of their tails.

I told Glenn a story my father had told me, about he and my Uncle Jim fishing the river near here when Jim was maybe 13 years old. Jim had stripped naked and dived underwater to retrieve a snagged lure and was climbing back up on the bank, when from around the bend came a flotilla of canoes filled with Girl Scouts. Jim yelped and jumped into the river, then sat up to his neck in the water while the girls drifted past one after another grinning at him.

We pushed on, taking our time. The day was too hot for hurrying. At one point we spotted another northern pike, this one tight to the bank. It hovered motionless, its shadow drawn sharply on the sand beneath it. I swung a streamer past it, but the fish didn't react. I pumped the fly to make it look alive, like an injured minnow maybe, an easy meal. But I got careless and let it get too close to the fish. It lodged against its pectoral fin.

The pike swirled and shot downstream. It was bigger than it had first appeared, maybe six or seven pounds. It ran beneath a tangle of submerged roots and rubbed the fly off.

Glenn was watching from a short distance upstream. "What happened?" he asked.

"You don't want to know."

By then the sun was getting low, and we were becoming tired and very thirsty. We didn't know how far it was to the bridge. I guessed we were only halfway. But I had a trick up my sleeve.

In many places the Crystal's meanders are so extreme that they nearly touch. You can step over a narrow neck of land and bypass a quarter mile of river. I knew this because I'd been fishing and canoeing the Crystal all my life and considered myself something of an expert. Also I remembered a day many years ago when my family and I paddled the river, my brother and I in one canoe, our parents in another. Rick and I had raced to get ahead of our folks, and were feeling pretty satisfied with ourselves. Then we came around a bend and there were Mom and Dad ahead of us, sitting casually in their canoe waiting for us to catch up. They had pulled the boat over a spit of land separating two bends of the river.

Now, employing the same tactic, I led Glenn up an eroded sandy cut and into the woods. It was an easy walk, less than a hundred yards. When we came out to the river and set off downstream again, I was smug with the knowledge that I had shortened our trip considerably.

We waded along, talking as we went, no longer bothering to fish. After a half hour or so Glenn said, "Didn't we already pass that tree?" He pointed at a cedar leaning into the river. Its top half had been cut off by a chainsaw to open the way for canoes and kayaks. Half a bend later we passed the pool where I'd snagged the pike and, a short distance beyond it, the sandy bank I had led us across for a shortcut. It was disorienting. Later, looking at a map at home, I noticed a cloverleaf of bends among the meanders, so maybe what I thought was an ordinary bend was a bend within a bend. Or a meander within a meander. Or something like that. It's still not clear to me. All I know is we somehow managed to go in a circle, which many wise and thoughtful people say is representative of our general course in life but is pretty damned unusual for a river.

We got back to the car about dark and drove to Art's Bar in search of further perspectives on the human dilemma.

Getting lost in a place I've known all my life was a little embarrassing, but that's okay. I've done much worse. Besides, blunders like that can be good for us. They knock us down a notch or two and reminds us that we're humble travelers in a complicated world.

River Rush

My old friend Norris McDowell and I were driving back roads in the Upper Peninsula, supposedly looking for places to hunt but mostly just enjoying the ride. Late in the afternoon, when the sun was getting low and we'd entered that period of intense light that photographers call the magic hour, we looked across a meadow to a wooded hill that was awash with brilliant reds and oranges—an insane burst of autumn colors. At the foot of the hill stood a magnificent whitetail deer with a rack of broad, thick-tined antlers. While I scrambled in the glove compartment for binoculars, Norris shook his head in wonder and said, "I love October. It's so damned arrogant."

Arrogant is right—and full of possibilities. There's so much to do that it's always a challenge to squeeze as much as you can from this richest month of the year.

For me a few October traditions can't be missed. Bird camp with my buddies, a cherished tradition since the mid-1980s. Wading rivers for late-season browns or early-season steelhead. Casting for walleye at dusk on Long Lake. But though there are never enough days to do everything I want, I try to devote at least one to the last canoe trip of the year. Some years it's the best day of all.

This ritual goes back to the spring of 1984, when Craig Date and I set out to canoe the lengths of nearly fifty Michigan rivers and write the book that would become *Canoeing Michigan Rivers*. We were very young then and very ambitious, with absolutely no idea what we were getting ourselves into. Like many young people, we were able to accomplish difficult tasks despite our ignorance—or maybe because of it. We thought this particular task would be easy: canoe a couple rivers every weekend and finish the book by Christmas, then sit back and watch the royalty checks roll in. It would take us six months, we figured. Eight at most.

Two and a half years later we paddled around a bend on the Shiawassee River and saw Craig's red truck parked on the bank and realized our work was done. By then we had canoed more than 1,500 miles together and were a little older and maybe even a little wiser. Our relief that the journey was over was exceeded only by our disappointment that it was over. Even then we knew that we would always look back on the experience as a momentous time in our lives.

As it turned out, not only those years but all the years since have been pretty momentous, in no small part because of running water. To my mind, Michigan rivers are the loveliest and most interesting in the world. Each has aromas, colors, velocity, and surrounding terrain that add up to make it unique. For years I was convinced that I could be blindfolded and led to any Michigan river and know exactly where I was.

River people know what I'm talking about. We're a tribe. We can never cross a bridge without looking for the water below it. We believe the meander is the most beautiful geometric form. We can't imagine why anyone would value the shortest distance between two points.

One of the great appeals of canoeing and kayaking is the freedom they offer. Freedom from a power source other than your muscles. The freedom to put a boat into the water, anywhere you choose, unlicensed and unregulated, and go as far as you want. Freedom to explore new places. Freedom from schedules and obligations. Freedom even from the need to paddle: On a river you can let the current do the work, giving you a free ride on the merry-go-round.

In a lifetime on the water, I've never gotten over my astonishment that a river flows, seemingly without end, and that we can flow along with it. I still get excited every time I push off from the bank. I still can't resist the draw of that first downstream bend and whatever waits beyond it. One thrust of my paddle and I'm lost in the swirling current, the red and green hills reflecting on the water, the maple leaves drifting on the surface.

Is there a better way to dance with arrogant October?

Bird Camp Memories

One surprise for me as I've grown older has been discovering that the farther from home you explore, the bigger your home becomes. Mine includes a place where I've gone nearly every October since 1986 to join up with old friends for a week of upland bird hunting. For fifteen years we camped in tents and got to know intimately the broad spectrum of northern Michigan's autumn weather. Then we grew a little tired of being wet and cold so we rented an eight-bedroom lodge with comfortable beds, hot water, and a spacious, superbly equipped kitchen. There was even a satellite dish and a large-screen television, though we turned it on only for Lions games and the World Series. The hunting nearby could be spotty, so some years a few of us left our shotguns in our rooms and went fishing. But "camp" has always been about much more than hunting and fishing.

For obvious reasons I can't be specific about location. I was introduced to the original camp in 1986, and promptly made the atrocious greenhorn mistake of writing about it in an article for the newspaper sometimes referred to as "The Gray Lady." The next year, to my horror, the woods were overrun by a distressing number of hunters driving vehicles with New York license plates. They raced at high speed along our two-tracks, poached our best hunting spots, and hogged all the tables in the diners.

Eventually my friends forgave me, though they remind me every year that I'm still on probation.

Anyway, Bird Camp has become one of the longest-standing annual traditions in my life. Here are some memories:

1. A Fall of Woodcock

It had to be the fog that kept the birds in the air that morning. A warm front had moved up from the south and settled in the Upper Peninsula, making it seem more like August than October, a condition that we've noticed occurring more and more as the years pass. But there were birds in the woods. Not big numbers of them, but enough to keep us hunting.

Hank, Doc, Tim, and I wanted to hunt the clear-cut we call the Church Cover, but because of the fog we decided to make another pot of coffee and stay in camp an extra hour. Finally around nine o'clock we loaded up and drove to the little white church, turned onto the two-track across from it, followed the trail to the aspen cover, parked, and let the dogs out of their crates. We loaded our guns and set off walking down the trail that cut through the aspens.

The fog still lingered, looking a little like a thick layer of clouds that had gotten snagged in the trees. It seemed to make the dogs uneasy. They stayed close to our feet as we walked.

Hank wasn't having any of it. He sent his German shorthair, Bell, into the shin-tangles. She's a dynamo, never quits. But now she darted in, made a tight circle, and returned to Hank's feet. He stared at her and said, "Hey." She glanced up and seemed to shrug. You could see the conviction in her eyes. "No birds in there, Boss."

Then we saw our first woodcock.

It fluttered down through the fog forty feet ahead. Doc's shorthair, Luc, saw it, too. He ran halfway and locked on point. We walked up and the bird flushed wild, but it barely cleared the ferns before it dropped to the ground again.

"That's a tired bird," Doc said.

Then another fluttered down.

And another.

Luc and Bell both went on point. We split up and approached the dogs and when we stepped in front of them the birds launched. But again they came up just above the understory, fluttered ahead a dozen feet, and dropped to the ground. Doc and Hank leashed their dogs and we stood on the trail and watched.

Through the fog thirty feet away a woodcock came down soundlessly through the white. Another emerged from overhead and landed two feet in front of startled Luc's nose. I counted about a dozen in all, though Hank would later claim we saw hundreds drop out of the sky that morning, and that if we had held our hands out we could have caught them like pop flies in the outfield.

Falls of woodcock were mentioned in print as early in the 15th century. *The Book of Saint Albans* lists it as a collective noun on par with "a gaggle of geese" and "a bevy of quails." Other old texts link it metaphorically with a fall of snow. The contemporary writer Tom Huggler, in his splendid *A Fall of Woodcock*, says the term disappeared from general use about 1430. Tom is the founder of our bird camp, a good friend, and we've all read his book, so naturally we've discussed the phenomenon many times. Woodcock tend to be solitary, and do not flock, so the chances of seeing them fall like snow is remote even under the best circumstances. "A fall of woodcock" is a colorful term of venery—and a fine title for Tom's book—but long ago we decided it had to be a biological myth.

And yet, here they were, falling from the sky. Ten, eleven, twelve woodcock fluttering down around us, some only a few strides away. Surely there were others that we didn't see.

They must have circled above the fog, weary from flying all night, until finally they were so exhausted that they had no choice but to plunge into that white sea. It was pure luck that four men and two dogs were there to see them parachute safely to the ground.

2. *A Double Between Two Rivers*

Tom Carney worries that he misses too many easy shots on grouse and woodcock. I don't know if he does or not; I miss plenty myself, so I'm in no position to judge. But I remember a day when his wing-shooting—— and his luck—turned stellar.

It was long ago, and I was new to upland hunting, yet the moment remains vivid in my memory. It was a perfect October day in the cover we came to call The Place Between Two Rivers—the sky blue, the air cold and crisp, the woods so quiet we could hear each aspen leaf as it fell to the ground around us. We had flushed a few woodcock and shot a couple but had not yet stumbled into the concentrations of flight birds that for the next five or six years would make this cover legendary among the members of our hunting camp.

At one point, as we elbowed through a thicket of young aspen, I asked Tom if he had ever shot a double on woodcock. I had been reading everything I could find about upland bird hunting and was starting to appreciate its lore and traditions but was still young enough to think a day's success could be measured by the number of birds in a game bag. If a double on grouse was a mark of great skill—and all the hunting authors agreed it was—then why not try for a double with woodcock?

Tom explained that woodcock are solitary by nature and therefore double flushes are exceedingly rare. He'd never doubled on woodcock. In fact, he didn't know anyone who had.

Those words had hardly left Tom's mouth when his English setter, Paddy, locked on point in front of us. Paddy was one the finest dogs I've ever hunted with, the epitome of what my father and uncles meant when they praised a dog as being "crackerjack." When Paddy went on point it was almost certain that he had pinned a bird. We walked in, and up burst two woodcock in a flurry of wings and whistles, launching in opposite directions.

Tom swung and fired, then swung and fired again.

Bang, bang, and he had his double on woodcock. To this day, we have yet to see another.

3. That Time It Rained

We hardly knew what to do with ourselves. Here we were, stuck indoors during this week we look forward to all year. Some of us thought we should hunt anyway, the rain be damned. Life is short, and so is bird season. Why waste a day?

But mature heads prevailed. They prevail more and more often, these days. And it really did look hopeless—unrelenting, roof-thrumming, with an all-day gloom settling into every corner of the house. Even the dogs gave up. They lay curled on their rugs in front of the fireplace, dreaming of kibble and birds.

Dave, standing before a window streaming with rain on the outside and condensation on the inside, said, "If you don't like the weather, wait five minutes. Mark Twain said that."

Ron said, "I thought he said, 'It's not the heat. It's the humidity.'"

We made another pot of coffee. Whipped up a second breakfast, too. The first one had been hurried and kind of skimpy, oatmeal for some, dry cereal for others. This time it was eggs over easy, venison sausage, slabs of homemade bread so thick we had to hammer them into the toaster. We sat elbow-to-elbow at the long table and went at it. Pass the salt, pass the hot sauce. Pass the sausage before I perish of hunger. As we ate we discussed memorable breakfasts of the past. Lumberjack soufflés at Horseshoe Lake. Blueberry pancakes in Seney. I told them about Nute Chapman's opening-morning banquets in Onaway. Somebody mentioned Steve's sky-high apple pie served with wedges of sharp cheddar on the side, and everybody got dreamy.

We cleared the table. Did the dishes. Moved to the living room. Tom C. sat in a recliner and patiently removed burs from his dogs' coats, placing them in a heap on the arm of his chair as he worked. Norris wandered over, paused to discuss the mysterious magnetism that draws burs to dogs, and walked off with a fist-sized nest of them clinging to his sleeve.

Cleaned our guns.

Oiled our boots.

The two Toms spread maps on the pool table and circled clear-cuts to investigate tomorrow.

Made lunch. Leftover lasagna and a tossed salad. Sat elbow-to-elbow at the table and tucked in. Pass the parmesan. Pass the garlic bread. Remember that lunch in the parking lot of the supermarket in Republic in 1991? Remember the time Ron built a mountainous sandwich to take to the woods with him and bragged and bragged about it, declaring it the Mightiest Sandwich in the History of the World, and when he went to the bathroom Jerry stole it? That was a mean thing to do, but kind of funny. Ron, did you ever forgive him? Nope. But remember, revenge is a dish best served cold.

Went to our separate corners and read. Harrison, McGuane, McCarthy, Proulx. A strange novel by that Japanese guy who puts monkeys in every book. The first volume of memoirs by the chain-smoking Norwegian whose struggles are so mundane they're somehow riveting.

Napped.

Cleaned the kitchen again.

Passed around a box of Rita treats and congratulated Randy for marrying her.

Discussed plans for dinner.

Got the cards out. Some cribbage. Some euchre. Tried getting a poker game going but Jim said he was tired of cards. Said cards are the ignorant person's substitute for conversation.

Dan said, "Okay. What do you want to talk about?"

Jim paused. "I don't know, what do *you* want to talk about?"

Silence.

"Deal the goddamned cards!"

Tim cracked open the bottle of Pappy Van Winkle he had saved for us since Christmas. It was the good one, the 23-year Family Reserve. Everybody had a taste. Everybody had another taste.

Tried to open a discussion about postmodernism in film and literature. Made poor progress. Hank suggested we never discuss it again. Norris seconded the motion.

Told stories. The morning at Witbeck Rapids with a foot of snow on the ground and flight birds everywhere. The day we discovered Triple Limit. The day we found The Place Between Two Rivers. The night at Horseshoe Lake when we were awakened in our tents by the screams of an axe murderer but it turned out to be Norris having a nightmare. Norris denies it to this day. "Wasn't me," he says, every time it comes up.

Had another taste of Winkle. Doc opened a bottle of single malt so we could see how the new and old worlds compare.

Some of us went outside, where we sat on deck chairs under the porch roof, sipping whiskey and smoking cigars while watching the rain slanting down.

Some of us joined Steve in the kitchen to help with dinner. His menu for tonight was chicken piccata with lemon-and-caper sauce, chicken liver pate with figs and walnuts, wild mushroom soup, blueberry cobbler.

Later, as we sat around the big dining room table about to begin eating, Tom H. raised his glass and said, "Here's to good friends, good books, and Steve's unforgettable dinners."

About three of us shouted at once, "Mark Twain said that!"

4. Be Prepared

One afternoon, while we were driving a two-track deep in Marquette County looking for bird cover, Tom Carney and Tim Roth fell into a deep discussion of situational ethics and how to lead a more principled life. Tom quoted Seneca—"The test of gold is fire; man, adversity"— words of special relevance to us because we kept meeting adversity in the form of trees that had fallen and blocked our way. Also the two-track kept meandering in unpredictable directions, none of which matched the ant trails in our map book. I don't know how many miles of two-tracks there are in northern Michigan, but we did our best to drive all of them that day.

When Tom shifted the truck into four-wheel and started to maneuver around a fallen tree instead of facing the adversity head-on, I recited a Mexican proverb: "Honor does not scuttle sideways like a crab."

Tom suggested that if I was so determined to be honorable I should fetch the bucksaw and cut the damned tree out of the way.

It was a big maple. About twenty inches across at the trunk. I decided that in this case, at least, it was okay to scuttle a little.

Tim observed that we were exercising the most famous principle of the Boy Scouts, "Be Prepared." That made us feel pretty good about ourselves because one thing we were was prepared. We had the bucksaw, three reliable compasses, one unreliable map book, a couple phones with GPS function that couldn't pick up a satellite signal, and a cooler filled with venison sausage and Widow Maker. All we had to do now was find a paved road and we'd be golden.

We came around a bend and discovered our way was blocked by a flooded beaver meadow. If the water was too deep to cross we would have to backtrack for miles. Then we noticed that midway in the flooding was a station wagon submerged to its fenders. Through binoculars we saw it had an Illinois license plate. Kneeling in the water next to it was a man in his thirties or forties shoving beaver sticks under the tires for traction. Standing beside him and watching us intently was a boy. He appeared to be about twelve years old.

We stepped out of the truck and walked to the edge of the flooding, and Tom shouted across to ask if we could be of assistance. We had a tow cable in the back of the truck. If we could get close enough it would be easy to hook up to the car and tow it to higher ground. The man gave no indication that he had heard him, so Tom called again, louder, "Can we give you a hand?"

Even from fifty yards away we could see the relief on the boy's face. He lit up like a floor lamp. But before he could say anything the man jumped to his feet and shouted back at us, "Heck no! We can get ourselves out! We love this stuff!"

We shrugged. The boy watched us forlornly. As we started to turn away and leave, the man called out, "Hey wait a second! Do you know where we are?"

"Nope!" we shouted, and everybody laughed. Everybody except the boy. He didn't find it funny at all.

Two-Trackin'

Two-tracks are everywhere in Michigan's wooded north. Many of them—probably the majority of them—began as logging trails hewed during the timber frenzy of the late 19th and early 20th centuries, when the harvest of Michigan's pines and hardwoods was worth more than all the gold mined in California. Some probably started much earlier as wildlife trails, were enlarged by human feet, and eventually became wide enough to accommodate horses and wagons. In all, there must be thousands of miles of them. How many is up for debate. I recently made the question public on social media and received a wide range of responses. A commercial logger insisted there were enough to circle the globe at the equator. An executive in the automobile industry claimed there were enough to reach the moon but probably not enough to return home. A rather embittered public servant temporarily employed in Lansing harangued tirelessly against two-tracks in general and said he planned to introduce legislation that would have them bulldozed, paved over, and made "useful." Thomas McGuane once said that if the trout disappear we should smash the state. I'd add two-tracks and hiking trails to that call to arms.

We probably wouldn't be talking about two-tracks at all if it wasn't for Michigan's wealth of public land. It's there that the trails have endured rather than being paved or plowed under. The state and national forests that were the original domain of giant white and red pines and massive oaks, beech, and maple, have remained forested, for the most part, with third- or fourth-generation trees standing as tribute to their majestic ancestors. These days hunters, anglers, mushroom pickers, lost wanderers, and occasional outlaws make use of the old trails, and in the process keep them unobstructed. Whenever a trail stops being used underbrush and trees move in to reclaim it, as they should.

When I was a kid one of my favorite things to do was explore two-tracks with my father in his war-surplus Jeep. I don't think Dad ever licensed it, on the theory that if he never drove it on pavement a license wasn't required. Maybe he was right, but I suspect not. All I know is that whenever I saw him walking toward the battered yellow war-machine in the backyard, I ran and jumped into the passenger seat. Then he'd fire up the engine, shift into first gear, and we'd be off and running. The Jeep shivered and bucked in every gear and had a top end of maybe 40 miles per hour but we hardly ever went that fast.

We had to drive only a mile or two from our home on Long Lake to reach the first two-track, then could make our way across entire counties without crossing more than a couple paved roads. If it had rained recently Dad would send me forward to test the bottom of mud puddles with a stick to make sure there was a substrate of gravel, then he would drive through in four-wheel drive. On special days he would allow me to sit behind the wheel, yank the floor shifter with both hands, grind into first gear and then second, and drive a half-mile down a stretch of two-track. In winter we followed the same trails on snowmobiles, sometimes teaming up with friends to caravan thirty miles to Honor to eat burgers and fries for dinner and returning home before midnight.

I had plans for my father's Jeep. The day I graduated from high school I would load it with extra cans of gasoline and oil, a shovel, an axe, a chainsaw, and other necessary gear, strap a canoe on top, and drive north to the Hudson Bay country. When I had gone as far as any trails would take me I would load my gear into the canoe and paddle north until I found a perfect homestead beside the water. Then I would build a log cabin and spend the rest of my life fishing and hunting every day in summer and fall and tending the woodstove and reading books all winter.

I never got possession of the Jeep—Dad sold it and bought a truck better capable of towing his fishing boat—but the ambition still haunts me. When I was in my thirties I met a kindred spirit in John Voelker, former Michigan Supreme Court Justice and author of *Trout Madness, Anatomy of a Murder,* and other books that are the most brilliant ever written about the Upper Peninsula. Voelker, who was in his eighties then, invited me into his Jeep Cherokee and led us on a long tour through the backcountry southeast of Ishpeming, ending up at his fishing camp on the beaver pond he referred to in his books as "Frenchman's Pond," though that's not its real name. Along the way he talked about fishing, books, ruffed grouse, and other subjects close to his heart and mine. He told me one reason he had remained in the U.P. most of his life was that he rarely needed to drive on pavement there. When we encountered an unavoidable few miles of highway, he solved the problem by cruising along the gravel shoulder at twenty miles per hour until he could dart onto the next two-track and breathe easily again.

I thought of Voelker not long ago when my wife and I spent a day exploring backcountry roads in the national forest near Munising with our friends Steve and Lori Tracey. I rode with Steve in his pickup, while Gail and Lori led the way in our SUV. It had rained the night before and every low spot on every two-track was flooded. At a puddle not much smaller than the beaver flooding where the man from Illinois got his station wagon stuck, Steve and I stopped and watched uneasily as Gail eased the car into the water. It got deeper and deeper, rising above the hubcaps, then to the fenders, and still Gail eased it forward. When she reached the point where it appeared the water would get no deeper, she accelerated aggressively, causing the car to push a bow wave big enough to surf on, and in a burst of spray launched onto dry land and braked to a stop. Instantly she and Lori raised their arms and howled in triumph. Wild Yooper women!

The Restless Season

What is this energy that floods our veins in autumn? When the nights start turning cold and the trees show their first reds and yellows, I rise at dawn and hurry outside to cut firewood and install storm windows, then rush off to spend the rest of the day fishing on rivers or hunting in the woods. Why so energetic? Why so restless?

Anthropologists say it might be because we're descended from nomads who followed the seasons in endless search of better hunting and foraging. We migrated on foot across continents, followed ice bridges to new lands, and when we butted up against oceans built boats and set off across the water. It's no wonder that we get fidgety when the days become short and the nights cold. It's our ancient selves whispering, "Go south, fool!"

Of course we're not the only ones to hear those whispers. As early as August monarch butterflies begin their epic migration to the mountains of central Mexico. Among the best places to observe them is along Great Lakes beaches. Early and late in the day, when the wind is down, you can sit on the beach and watch monarchs flutter steadily southward, one every minute or so, their flight erratic but resolute.

By October warblers are passing through on their way to the Deep South, the Gulf Coast, and beyond. These are not the brightly colored warblers of spring. They wear drab coats now, and it takes a practiced eye to know a pine warbler from a bay-breasted or a blackpoll.

Other birds are heading out, as well. I remember an unusually warm day in October in the western U.P. when I watched half a dozen hermit thrushes hopping across the ground in an aspen wood, flipping leaves in search of insects, moving constantly southward. I left the woods and turned onto a highway in my car. On the road ahead a flurry of leaves burst into the air and transformed into a flock of snow buntings, their white wings flashing in unison. During the drive home, the weather turned, and by the time I reached the Straits of Mackinac a harsh wind rattled sleet against the windshield. On the water on both sides of the bridge were vast rafts of ducks—redheads, mostly, as well as some scaup, canvasbacks, and goldeneyes—so many that in their massed thousands they undulated on the waves like floating carpets the size of football fields.

When I was a kid I loved the migration season because it meant the summer people were going home and the lake would be mine again. I went out in our aluminum rowboat and cast Mepps spinners into glass-calm bays, the surface reflecting the oranges and yellows of hardwoods along the shore. At night, lying in bed, I would listen to the honking of geese as they passed overhead, bound for their winter grounds far to the south. It was the melancholy song of autumn, and it made my heart beat faster and my blood flow stronger. It still does. Some days I wouldn't mind taking wing and following the geese south, but usually I'm quite content to stay here and see what comes next.

A November Wind

That evening, when the wind started banging against the windows of our house, I put on my coat and drove to the foot of West Grand Traverse Bay to watch the waves.

A dozen people were there already, sitting in cars in the parking lot at Clinch Park. From the darkness came steep and ragged waves as big as houses. They charged toward us and smashed against the breakwall, the impact throwing geysers of spray twenty feet into the air. The wind caught the spray and blew it to shore, over the cars with their windshield wipers slapping, over the parking lot and the lawn beyond it, entering the city and washing away the illusion that civilization is a fortress that separates us from nature. We've always known the separation is tenuous. The walls are fragile and easily breached by waves and blizzards, by hail and flood, by crows, coyotes, mosquitoes, and mice, by our own untamed natures.

Traverse City, like most of the towns and cities around the Great Lakes, was built with its back to the water. The city founders had turned away from an embarrassment. For decades they thought nothing of dumping their garbage and sewage into the bay and the river that flows into it. I'm old enough to remember when Traverse City's beaches were heaped with cherry pits and household trash, and the Boardman

River flowed soupy green and carried a stench of chemicals and decay through the center of town. You can hear similar stories all around the Great Lakes.

There is much yet to do, but we've made progress in recent decades. Many cities have vitalized their waterfronts, allowing them to turn around and face the water. Industries can no longer dump their wastes in the lakes, and our sewage systems, though barely adequate at best and subject to overflow every time there's a major rain event, are better than they were. Most of us now understand a truth that was hidden for decades: Our lakes and rivers are owned by everyone, and it is within our power to do whatever is necessary to protect them from those who would use them carelessly and selfishly.

I suspect many of us long ago intuited this idea of common ownership, although we might be more comfortable thinking of ourselves not as owners, but custodians. The Great Lakes are too big to be owned. They remain the last great wilderness of the middle continent—unsettled, uncultivated, vast. Every effort to possess or tame them has always been defeated.

For a people so well supplied with information, we're awfully starved for wisdom. But here's a bit of wisdom I sensed that night when Lake Michigan seemed determined to tear Clinch Park apart, stone by stone: We are puny. We are temporary. We can talk until our voices crack, but the wind and water will always speak louder.

Winter

Winter Roads

My son Nick and I were driving home one afternoon when we came upon a car stuck in a snowbank. It was a snow-globe kind of day, with millions of big flakes falling so heavily that we could watch them piling up on fence posts and telephone wires, as well as on the road. The driver of the car had evidently intended to turn onto a side road but must have been going a little too fast for conditions, for his car had slid through the intersection and plowed into the bank. A man in a formal suit and tie stood thigh-deep in the snow, pushing against the front of the car, while the driver accelerated the engine until it roared and spun the wheels to no effect.

Nick and I pulled over to offer our assistance. As we approached the driver, who turned out to be a young man in a tuxedo, he leaned from the side window and explained with some urgency that he and his father were on their way to a wedding, *his* wedding, and they were already late. The ceremony was being held at a vineyard a mile down the side road.

Winter isn't exactly the high time for outdoor weddings around here, but they are not uncommon in wine country. The landscape is picturesque, the hills picketed with rows of vine posts rising above the snow and bordered by patchwork woods and orchards. Throw in the romance of wine-making and the charming idea of *terroir*, and it's a fine place to start building memories.

If one of those memories is being late for your wedding because you and your dad got stuck in a snowbank, so much the better. You'll be telling the story for the rest of your life.

Nick and I joined the groom's father at the front of the car, got it rocking, and helped push it back onto the road. It's what people do in winter—help one another meet the perils and challenges of icy roads, dangerous windchill, and frozen water pipes.

But we were aware that more was involved this time. We were helping nudge a young man into his future. It was waiting for him, just down the road, with all its joys and hardships to come. We watched him drive toward it eagerly, he and his father waving to us from their windows. Nick and I grinned at each other and climbed back into our car. Ahead was our own road, snow-covered and slippery, and we were ready for whatever awaited us along the way.

Winter and White Space

In winter it's easier to notice the little things. Maybe a clump of snow falling from a hemlock bough. Maybe a redpoll at the bird feeder. Maybe the shimmering snow crystals called "diamond dust" that sometimes, on very cold days, drift down from a blue sky.

For years Gail and I have been trying to simplify our lives so that we might become more aware of such things, but we haven't made much headway. The effort always makes me think of Thoreau, in *Walden*, where he famously scolded us to "simplify, simplify," then proceeded to weave a deliciously complex tapestry of a book. It's as it should be. The most enduring books, like natural communities, are made stronger by their complexity. Those tens of thousands of words in intricate arrangement focus our attention, expand our view of the world, and remind us that we're surrounded every moment by an unimaginable abundance of things. That words can perform such magic is astonishing. Surely it is our greatest achievement. Sometime in the unimaginable past our ancestors began constructing words and stuffing the universe inside them, and we've been passing them around like lockets ever since. Crack them open and out spill snowflakes and blue jays, the scent of apricots, laughing children—all the sensation-packed moments that add up to become a life.

Maybe we seek the spare and elemental in nature for the same reason that the protagonist in Don DeLillo's *Cosmopolis* reads poetry: "He liked spare poems sited minutely in white space . . . Poems made him conscious of his breathing." What if the simple life exists only in the space between things? In a space where we can be conscious of our breathing? In language so ventilated it lets light and oxygen in? Maybe the simplicity we've been seeking could free us from some of the clamor and clutter of the human world and grant us entry into a place like the one Elizabeth Gilbert seeks in *The Signature of All Things*: "I would like to spend the rest of my days in a place so silent—and working at a pace so slow—that I would be able to hear myself living."

But of course we're not simple creatures. Bare moments can't hold us for long. Eventually we require more than white space and cloud spout; more than the twice-warming fire in a woodstove; more than the monkish austerity of a small room, a candle, and a few books. Thoreau's enthusiasm is infectious—"Think of our life in nature . . . rocks, trees, wind on our cheeks! The solid earth! the actual world! the common sense! Contact! Contact!"—but I suspect we're more interested in his boldness and passion and the intricacies of his mind than in the simple life he championed. The louder and more eloquently Thoreau crowed in praise of simplicity, the more convincing became his argument against it.

Yet there's the winter landscape.

It snowed last night, a heavy snow that made the field behind our house an expanse of white space. Not perfect, though: a few stems of knapweed and goldenrod rose above it. They marked the snow like ink scratches on a sheet of paper, forming the sparest of poems—a letter "i" near the top of the page, a hyphen in the middle, a comma at the bottom. I almost couldn't bring myself to spoil it.

But I did. I set off across the field in my clumsy boots, thinking of this and that—just another careless biped passing through—and left a meandering trail that will be there until the next good snow erases it.

The Quiet Hours

Years ago, when the boys were young and we lived in our little house in the Old Town neighborhood of Traverse City, we often walked to the Carnegie Library on Sixth Street. After dinner on winter evenings we would bundle up in our coats, boots, hats, and mittens and set out through the snow. If it had stormed that day and the night was very cold and the plows hadn't reached our neighborhood yet, there would be no traffic and we would enjoy the novelty of walking down the center of the street, breaking trail through the new snow. When we looked back the way we had come, Gail's and my tracks were a straight line down the street. The boys' tracks wandered from side to side, for they were interested in everything, and everything required investigation.

The library was often busy those evenings. Cars would be parked at odd angles in the parking lot; deep ruts showed where vehicles had gotten stuck and had to be rocked free. We stepped inside to a festive atmosphere of rosy cheeks and laughter, everyone bumped out of their ordinary selves by the storm. We felt fortunate to be in that warm, bright space, surrounded by people who shared our appreciation. The library has never seemed a greater haven of light and hope.

I was reminded of those evenings not long ago, when a winter storm closed our little city for a couple of days. It was one of those storms that people complain about but secretly find energizing. Schools and government offices closed, and most of us enjoyed a time-out.

Late on the second night, while the storm was winding down, I took a walk down Front Street. The downtown district was deserted and so quiet that it seemed I must be the only person in the city who was still awake. Drifts clogged the street and parked cars were heaped with so much snow it appeared as if they had been abandoned. The snow muffled all sound.

I've lived in Traverse City so long that every street and building is drenched with memories. I walked past Front Row Centre, where I rented an office in my early thirties while writing two books and part of a third, and which, during my childhood and until I was out of high school, was the Michigan Theatre, one of two movie theaters within a block of each other. It was where Gail and I went on our first date, to see *Jaws*. I remember standing in line with her laughing about the story in that day's newspaper about the decomposing carcass of a small shark that someone had discovered washed up on Clinch Park Beach, setting off a minor panic among swimmers. It took some time to convince them that it was a hoax.

Across the street from Front Row Centre is a restaurant, Poppycocks, in the space where Stacey's Restaurant used to be. Stacey's operated for decades on an eccentric principle: When you finished your meal you paid the bill by going to the cash register, ringing it open, and making the payment and collecting your change on the honor system. It's where I met Glenn Wolff for the first time, for lunch in 1988. By the end of that lunch we had sketched out the first book we would do together, *It's Raining Frogs and Fishes*.

As I broke trail on the street, I was joined by a stray dog, a long-haired mongrel that might have had some border collie in him. He approached, stopped a few feet away, and we made eye contact. I swear he nodded in recognition—"Can't sleep? Well then, let's walk"—and we set off together, past streetlights with snowflakes flaring beneath them and the darkened storefronts with their windows etched with frost. It was like seeing my hometown for the first time. At night, deserted, it seemed a different place altogether. We often think of the daylight hours as the conventional part of the day, where order and reason rule,

and there is safety. Night is unconventional, intuitive, slightly dangerous. Walk a city at night in a snowstorm and you'll see those qualities
intensified.

And isn't that one of the pleasures of a storm? How it shakes us
from our routines and forces us to pay closer attention to the world?

Ken Scott's Ice Caves

On a Sunday afternoon in March, Gail and I followed photographer Ken Scott onto frozen Lake Michigan and discovered that we had the Leelanau ice caves to ourselves. We were surprised. One weekend a few weeks earlier an estimated 5,000 people were there, causing traffic jams in a corner of Leelanau County that most winters is traffic-free.

But the winter of 2013–14 was not like most winters. Ken loaned us his extra pairs of snowshoes equipped with steel cleats to grip the ice and led us down the trail from Gill's Pier Road. We shuffled across an ice field spangled with beach sand until we reached the humped and bulging back of ice formations rising so high they cut off our view of the lake. We descended through a steep chute between them and came out in front of the formations. Now we could see their scale: a great wall of ice fifteen to twenty feet high running the length of the shore as far as we could see. Along it were ramparts and parapets sculpted into shapes suggestive of the waves that had formed them. Some parts looked like faces in profile; some had the elephant and doughboy shapes of cumulus clouds; some were as sheer as the prows of ships.

Tucked in among them were the caves themselves: domed or key-hole shaped or vaulted like naves in a cathedral. A small cathedral, of course, but spacious enough for a dozen people to stand upright inside them. The floors were smooth and white, like melted candle wax. Overhead, the ceilings dripped with blue-tinted daggers of clear ice.

At one point Ken stopped and turned his head toward the big lake. In summer it would be blue water as far as we could see, with rollers breaking at our feet, but now all we could see was a jumbled sea of ice extending to the horizon. It could have been the frozen Arctic.

"Listen," Ken said. We listened but heard nothing. He grinned. "Last week the ice was groaning out there. It sounded like whales singing."

We were only a few weeks into the winter when we began to realize that it might turn epic. Even in December it reminded us of the winters of our childhood, when temperatures were often below zero and county plows could never quite clear the drifts. Then came February and the winter started to get epic indeed.

We woke every morning to temperatures below zero—15, 18, or 20 below. Day after day it snowed. Plows shoved it into banks along the highways so high they nearly touched power lines. Schools closed, sometimes for two or three days in succession. It became a Siberian winter, filled with sastrugi drifts.

A meteorological term entered our lexicon that year: polar vortex. The weather guy explained that the arctic jet stream was looping farther south than usual and with it came a circling mass of frigid air that usually stayed above Baffin Island and Siberia. It settled over the Great Plains and the Great Lakes region, bringing snowstorms and subzero temperatures. Most of the eastern half of the United States felt the bite. It wasn't just cold. It was the Arctic come down to visit. Records started falling; more schools closed.

The snow kept falling. Most winters there's a midwinter thaw or two, so even if a hundred inches of snow has fallen, only a couple feet will remain on the ground. But this year the snow didn't melt. It piled up. Michigan's Leelanau County got more of it than most places. Lake effect snow accumulates on most of the windward shores of the Great Lakes, but this year the Leelanau Peninsula—the little finger of the mitten—got much more than its share. Maple City made news when it received more snow than the Upper Peninsula's Keweenaw Peninsula.

It snowed until the roofs of buildings collapsed. It snowed until there was no place for the Road Commission to put it. People had to ease their cars into intersections and honk their horns to warn oncoming traffic because nobody could see around the banks.

And then the Great Lakes began to freeze. Not just the bays—that was rare enough—but the big water, the wide-open fetch. It had been years. Many of us remembered the winter of 1977–78, when storms paralyzed the continent from the Canadian prairies to New England. That year 93.1 percent of Lake Michigan froze over. It set a record many thought would stand forever. But 2014 broke the record—barely, but still—when 93.3 percent of the lake froze over.

It began early in December, with ice anchoring in the sand and gravel at the edges of the lake. Waves washed over it and froze, adding layers. A ledge formed—brilliant white because of the air trapped inside, and as smooth as wax from the waves washing over it.

The waves forced a way under the ice. You would see one break against the ledge and a moment later hear a deep bass throbbing as it passed through hollows underneath. If the water found a fissure it would rush through it to the surface and burst upward in a geyserlike spout. Spaced at intervals along the ledge, the spout-holes grew into cones of ice ten or fifteen feet high. A wave would strike—and a beat later a white volcano erupted.

Ledges grew into ramparts and castles. Waves shoved plates of blue ice the size of patios onto the ramparts, and breaking waves coated them in white. The waves were doing other work, as well. They burrowed into openings in the ice, excavating small chambers into bigger ones, enlarging and smoothing until they formed smooth-walled caves.

The caves were a surprise. Many of us had seen similar structures during other winters, but never so many of them, and never this large. These were big enough for a crowd of people to fit inside, and as elaborate as limestone caves. They were cellars and grottos. Wave spray had embellished them with columns and pillars. Their surfaces were so smooth they gleamed in sunlight, and from their ceilings dripped thousands of crystal stalactites.

Meanwhile the lake grew colder. The near-shore wash was thick with slush, with ice balls and plates banging against each other. Then it froze into aggregate. Farther out sheets of clear ice formed, but waves shattered them and the pieces joined the aggregate. A wasteland of jumbled ice grew to the horizon, around the islands, and across to Green Bay. It spread south, past the Manitous and Point Betsie, down the shore and across the widest spot in the lake—118 miles of open water to Wisconsin. And it froze as well around the southern end of the lake, for the temperatures in Chicago were as cold as they were in the north.

And during it all, the formations along the Leelanau coast became larger. In February news of the caves was picked up by television stations and newspapers, but the mainstream media had already been scooped by Facebook and Twitter. Traffic jams forced the sheriff to close Gill's Pier Road. After that people had to walk two miles to see the ice—and still they came by the hundreds. Many of them poured into Fischer's Happy Hour Tavern on M-22, where the hottest item on the menu was the Cave Burger.

The photos going around Facebook were stunning. Many of the most stunning were taken by Ken Scott. He was not the first to photograph the formations; he arrived after the rumors had already started circulating. I'm surprised that he wasn't the first one there. Not much happens outdoors in Leelanau County that Ken isn't on hand to photograph.

Once Ken saw the ice, he came back every day. Not from a sense of duty, but because it was fun. Ken earns his living with his camera—and works day and night, in every season, to do it—but he's never lost his spirit of play. He likes to place his camera on the ice, set the timer, then run to capture a photo of himself leaping against the sky.

He'll sit for hours waiting for the light to make some subtle switch, then fling himself into action. I've seen him dive to his belly to get a close-up of something on the ground, then roll over onto his back to examine what the sky looks like from that vantage. Now and then he spins in circles and cuts loose with wild, panoramic volleys from his camera, as if firing flowers at the world.

We're lucky to have him. And lucky that he was here to document the remarkable ice formations during this remarkable winter. I'm certain we'll be talking about this winter of ice and cold—and Ken Scott's artistry—for many years.

Star Matter

Not long ago I was walking with my dog in Martha's Woods, a couple miles from our home on Old Mission Peninsula. It was the first spring-like day of the winter, and though the crust was still frozen enough to support Toby's and my weight, it was growing softer in the rising warmth. The sky was the brittle blue of winter, but the breeze carried hints of spring.

As we walked I found myself thinking about the origins of the word "spring"—the springing forth of new growth, the greening of the earth as it leaps awake after a winter of sleep. Then, for some reason, I thought back to eighth-grade science class and remembered how surprised and thrilled I was to learn that we are composed of atoms that were once stellar refuse. Our constituent atoms, according to fierce Mr. Proulx, were thrown into space by exploding suns, then for billions of years congealed under forces not well understood to form asteroids, planets, moons, and interstellar dust. Matter. We too are matter, he said, composed of those same atoms and molecules. Thus we are made from stars and within us are the sparks of ancient electrons, with their snapping leaps across space. We are encapsulated energy. Even without astrophysics to confirm it, said Mr. Proulx, we long ago guessed our origin must be in the stars. It's to the sky we've always reached, after all, with our eyes and hands and cathedrals and skyscrapers. It's where we conceived heaven must be. We want to soar toward it, not anchor ourselves to the ground. We reach upwards, charting the trajectories of our achievements, successes, ranks, stardom. And everyone wants to be a star! We leap, we climb, we *aspire*—

—And at that moment I glimpsed a flash of orange through the trees and saw the fluid lope of a fox trotting in the field between the maple woods and the cherry orchard. Behind it trotted another. I had known from the tracks I had noticed all winter that a pair denned here, but this was the first I had seen them.

The lead fox disappeared into the woods while the other paused in the open and began searching in the snow with its head and tail down in that characteristic canid slouch. Perhaps it heard a vole scratching in a run beneath the snow. Then, with its head still down, it suddenly turned and began trotting toward me. The wind was in my face, so the fox was not likely to scent me or my dog. I was curious to see how close it would come, so I stood motionless, camouflaged, I imagined, by the trees at my back. But Toby trotted obliviously ahead. When he was thirty feet away he reached the end of his invisible tether and stopped, realizing that I was no longer following. He had not seen the fox. He was too occupied with the near-at-hand. Now he raced back, tongue lolling, an expression on his face that seemed like an embarrassed smile—"Stupid me! I wandered!" His eager gallop caused him to punch through the crust and threw his cadence off.

The fox disappeared behind a saddle of land. I assumed it would turn into the woods beyond my sight and rejoin its mate, so I stepped from the trees into the meadow. Suddenly the fox trotted into the open, so close that I could see its eyes widen when it saw us. It froze. I froze. Toby nosed the snow obliviously. The fox wheeled and ran to the woods, but it stopped at the edge of the treeline to look back. I think it was taking a second look at the dog. Toby's tawny coat contained hints of russet, making it distinctly foxlike, though he was more wolfish in size. After a moment the fox turned again and glided without sound into the woods, its magnificent brush floating behind.

My mind had gone empty, wiped clean by the encounter. For a moment I had slipped beneath the surface, between the chinks, to that timeless place before civilization, before even language.

But what was I thinking before the fox appeared? Something important . . . Oh yes, aspiration, ascent, star matter. But more as well, something articulated but lost in that fleeting encounter with the wild and the barter it had made for my attention. A good trade, surely, but I always regret what I've failed to notice, forgotten, lost . . .

Then it came back to me, a separate thought, hardly original but unusual because it had arrived in my mind fully formed: "Everything I do in my life, if it is to have significance, must be informed by the certainty of my death."

But why was I thinking it?

And what will I do with it?

Winter Time

It's an illusion, of course, but winter hours seem longer than summer hours. In June, when the days last from five in the morning until ten at night, there's hardly time to accomplish everything you want to do. But in winter, time languishes. You can work eight hours, plow the driveway, prepare dinner, eat, clean the kitchen, build a fire in the fireplace, read a book for an hour—and still have most of the evening ahead of you.

In the mornings, while I'm filling the bird feeders, a few black-capped chickadees converge even before I've finished and land inches from my hands. We lure birds into our yards because birds are wild and free and we want to be wild and free ourselves. This swinging feeder stocked with sunflower seeds draws birds we might otherwise notice only as distant, flitting, unidentified shadows in the trees. Drawn to our feeder, hopping from twig to twig to twig in the shrubs two feet outside our windows, the birds prove to be not indistinct Little Gray Units, but finches, juncos, redpolls—astonishing living beings brushed in colors and vivid details. A bird is the very embodiment of wildness. When it accepts our offerings of sunflower and suet, the space between us fills somehow.

Of course birds aren't the only wildlife we can watch in winter. Years ago a few friends and I would set off every winter on canoe and camping trips down rivers in northern Michigan that flowed fast enough to resist freezing over—usually the Pere Marquette, Pine, Manistee, or Au Sable. During those expeditions we would see dozens, sometimes hundreds of whitetail deer yarded in the cedar swamps, where they had churned the snow beneath the trees and trimmed the foliage to the precise height they could reach. The deer were unaccustomed to seeing humans at that time of year, so they behaved as if unobserved, nuzzling one another, rising delicately on their hind legs to strip cedar boughs with their teeth. We often drifted within a few feet of them when they were bedded on the banks and as long as we made no sudden movements they simply watched us, conserving their energy.

Sometimes otters swam near and raised themselves half out of the water for a look. One January we counted a dozen bald eagles during two days on the Au Sable River. We viewed them at close range, perched on pine branches above the river, eyeing us with interest as we drifted beneath. Often we saw pileated woodpeckers, and sometimes pairs of them. They dropped from the trunk of a dead tree, first one then the other, and soared away clumsily, seeming too heavy for flight, as if their bones were made of iron. Between every wing stroke they fell a few inches, rose again on the upbeat, then fell again. If they had missed a stroke they would have plunged to the ground like hatchets.

On winter days when I've had enough of staying indoors, I walk the woods and meadows near home to see what I can see. Often it's the tracks of hare, coyote, fox, and raccoon. Or, less commonly, pellets packed with fur and bones regurgitated by a barred owl and left in the snow beneath a basswood. Or, sometimes, evidence of drama, such as the snow-angel imprint where a hawk struck the snow, each feather as distinct as a fossil in shale, and beside it remnants of blood and fur from the vole that it preyed upon. When I slow down enough to notice such things, time slows as well. I can almost weigh it in my hands—can almost see the moments falling like snowflakes around me.

Waxwings in Winter

One day in the middle of cabin-fever season, Gail and I took a drive to get out of the house for a while. As we were heading out the door we grabbed our binoculars in case we happened across any interesting birds. We didn't expect any. The bird palette is quite limited in this season.

We drove to the end of the peninsula and explored stacks of ice floes that had been driven onto shore by the wind. Our first winter in our home on Old Mission, in 1991, we visited this spot with our young sons and saw a snowy owl perched on the ice, fifty yards offshore. It was the first snowy owl our sons had seen and a novelty for Gail and me.

This day there wasn't much to see but the ice, so Gail and I soon returned to the car and headed home. As we approached the Baptist church on Center Road we noticed flocks of birds flying in and out of trees beside the road. There was something unusual about them, so we wheeled into the driveway of the church and stepped out for a look.

What we saw became the birding highlight of the year. In the tops of the maples and birches on both sides of the road and especially in the big shade trees above the cemetery were hundreds of cedar and bohemian waxwings. We couldn't have been more surprised. Cedar waxwings are among our favorite songbirds, but we rarely see bohemians. They're common across northern Canada and not unusual in the U.P., but are only occasionally seen in the Lower Peninsula. These flocks were about evenly divided between the two species, with perhaps more bohemians than cedars. They were feeding ferociously on leaf buds in the maples and red berries in shrubs along the road.

Later, when we told our birder friends about the incident, they were surprised. The consensus was that frigid weather and a shortage of food in Canada and the U.P. had driven the birds south of the Mackinac Bridge, just as it did some years with snowy owls, northern goshawk, and other species from the far north. Nobody was surprised when we told them that the waxwings were gone the next day and that we had not seen them since.

Why did it thrill us? What is it about encountering uncommon wildlife that electrifies us? In winter it might be partly relief from routine. The buttery yellow and cream bellies of the cedar waxwings and the reddish undertail coverts of the bohemians—which makes them appear to have sat in raspberry juice—were like snack food for our famished eyes. It reminded me of a wonderful passage from Willa Cather's novel *My Ántonia*, about frontier life in Nebraska at the end of the 19th century: "In the winter bleakness a hunger for color came over people, like the Laplander's craving for fats and sugar. Without knowing why, we used to linger on the sidewalk outside the church when the lamps were lighted early for choir practice or prayer meeting, shivering and talking until our feet were like lumps of ice. The crude reds and greens and blues of that colored glass held us there . . ."

Biologists say we're hardwired to notice the unusual. It's how we survived for tens of thousands of years without rifles or refrigerators. We glimpsed the twitch of a sabertooth's ear through the underbrush and knew it meant danger. We saw spots of red on a hillside across the valley and knew it meant berries to eat.

That gray winter day Gail and I were famished not just for color, but for variety. When it came to us as an unexpected gift we did what any sensible person would do, tucked in and enjoyed the feast.

My Lost Lake

In winter I spend a ridiculous amount of time planning ahead to fishing in the summer. This habit goes back to when I was a kid sitting in class daydreaming about canoeing across Canada on waters that had never been fished and were full of hungry behemoths. I assumed by the time I reached manhood I would figure out how to do it for a living.

When I was 17, about to be booted out of high school and facing the prospects of either college or the draft, I stopped in one day to see Bob Summers, who's renowned in the fly-fishing world for the fine bamboo rods he builds by hand in his workshop on the Boardman River. I asked him if he had any idea how a promising young man could earn a living as a fisherman without having to work very hard. He perked right up. Turns out, he had just the thing for me. I could recruit a team of elderly people, he said, who were bored and would work for next to nothing, and teach them to tie artificial flies. But to make the venture profitable I would have to organize an assembly line. Each employee would specialize in a single part of the fly—body, wings, tail, or hackle—and would do that one small job a few thousand times a day. As long as the assembly line kept running I could go fishing whenever I wanted, and the money would pour in.

So I went to college. Quit when it got too difficult. Went to a different college. Quit again. Went to a third college, this one in Kentucky, far from distracting trout streams, and that time it stuck. After a few years I stepped into the wide, uncaring world with a diploma in my hand and asked, "What now?"

As so often when facing difficult decisions, I went fishing. At one point I found myself in the U.P. dragging my canoe through a tag-alder swamp about the size of Rhode Island. I was following directions I'd gotten from a guy I met across the pump at a gas station, but when I finally busted into the open, the pond before me didn't appear to be the one he had described. He had mentioned something about an island, and this pond had none. My heart started hammering when it occurred to me that I might have stumbled on water that had never been fished.

It was maybe five acres, hemmed around by tamaracks, with water so dark from tannin that the blade of my paddle disappeared a foot below the surface. And, oh, it was filled with brook trout. They attacked my artificial flies as if they had never seen such succulent baubles. What a discovery! My boyhood dreams had come true. I fished until dark, dragged my canoe through the alders to my car, and set out in search of a paved road.

When I returned the next summer to fish the pond again, I couldn't find it. Searched and searched. Found plenty of tag-alder swamps, some almost as big as Guam, but no pond. All these years later, I'm still searching.

And I'm fine with that. I'm just grateful to live in a place where it's possible to lose a lake.

Real Winter

There was a spell of harsh weather last winter that reminded me of the old days. It was cold—down to the single digits most days—and I spent much of my time in the living room feeding the fireplace and looking out the windows at the snow squalls howling down the road and filling the driveway with drifts. We were snowed in for days, though, I admit, we didn't try very hard to get out.

I remembered similar days in other recent winters. During a stormy period in March 2019, for instance, my friend Jim Ekdahl, who lives at the base of the Keweenaw Peninsula, sent a photo of his son and some friends shoveling snow from the roof of a cabin in Marquette County's McCormick Tract. The McCormick is in the heart of Superior's lake-effect zone and gets some of the heaviest snowfalls east of the Rockies. The young men were carving blocks of snow from an accumulation as high as their heads. It was reminiscent of vintage photos of winters in Michigan a century ago. Those were the years of what my grandfather used to refer to as *real* winters.

But they might not be a relic of the past. Climatologists predict that as global temperatures rise and the waters of the Great Lakes become warmer, we'll see increasingly severe storms, especially on the windward shores, where the heaviest loads of lake-effect snow fall. We could be in for many "real" winters in the years to come.

Already we're relying on superlatives to describe them. It was only a few years ago that the term "polar vortex" entered the popular lexicon. About that time a meteorologist went viral on social media with what she called the "Misery Index"—the combination of low temperature, heavy snowfall, strong winds, and extended periods of overcast skies that can make northerners abandon their homes and hightail it south. She concluded that the Misery Index for the winter of 2014 was the highest since 1950.

One especially cold day in February 2018 Gail and I drove north to Petoskey to visit Gail's sister Karen and her husband, Tim. In the scenic stretch of US-31 that borders Lake Michigan as you approach Little Traverse Bay, we saw the lake in an unusual mode. Waves rose and fell sluggishly, like a slushee tipping back and forth in a bowl, the water so viscous it was surely on the verge of freezing. The waves, cobalt blue and shimmering with ice crystals, had shoved millions of ice balls the size of oranges against the ledge ice along shore. We wanted to take photos, but the shoulder of the highway hadn't been plowed and there was no safe place to pull over. All we could do was watch as we drove by.

That winter we burned fifty percent more heating oil than usual, and twice as much fireplace wood. I shoveled snow off the roof every morning to prevent ice damming and for thirteen days in a row had to clear the driveway of drifts so high they sometimes collapsed onto the snowblower and stalled the engine. I thought of my grandfather, Clair Dennis, a cherry farmer in Leelanau County, and imagined he would have been proud to see me battling through another real Michigan winter.

Then I remembered how content that stalwart, uncomplaining veteran of Michigan's winters was to spend his final ones in Florida.

Visitors

In the morning we woke to a new world. The storm had filled the driveway with waist-high drifts and the road beyond was unplowed and impassable. Schools were closed, of course. It appeared that nobody was going to work, either.

Later, after I had cleared the driveway and the county plow had opened Blue Water Road, we drove to Mapleton to stock up on groceries. Half a mile from home we saw a snowy owl perched at the top of a telephone pole. It was the seventh day in a row we had seen her on that same pole. We pulled over and shut off the engine and watched through binoculars. She was almost pure white, and huge—that was how we knew she was female. As we watched, she turned her head nearly all the way around to look at us and blinked one yellow eye, then the other. Then she dropped from the pole and soared low across the meadow without once flapping her wings. Her wingspan looked to be five feet, at least. And in flight her coloring became even more brilliant, brighter even than the snow—so bright she seemed to be a source of light. I've never seen a more magnificent bird.

The summer people went home long ago, but we still get visitors. Snowy owls are among those we look forward to most every year. They arrive in January or February, driven from the Arctic tundra when lemmings and other prey are scarce. Some years we see none. Other years so many show up that they constitute what wildlife biologists call an "irruption." During an irruption a few years ago a dozen or more took up residence in Grand Traverse and Leelanau counties, where they had apparently found enough snowshoe hares, meadow voles, and mice to support them. Hundreds of others continued on and at least one made it as far south as Texas. Locally one big female chose to roost on a rooftop a block from downtown Traverse City and stayed for many days. She became a celebrity of sorts and built a strong presence on social media.

On a Saturday night during that same winter a few friends and I had dinner at one of our favorite downtown restaurants, Amical. We lingered over the meal, talking and drinking wine, and ended up closing the place. The owner, Dave Denison, joined us for a final glass of wine and we got talking about the weather, which in this case was not idle talk. The night was bitterly cold, well below zero, and the streets and sidewalks were deserted. Homeless people who usually came to the back door of the restaurant to receive the packages of leftovers that Dave's staff prepare for them every night had not shown up. We hoped they were sleeping in warm rooms at the homeless shelter.

Dave had a sudden inspiration and filled a coffee mug with boiling water from the kitchen. We followed him outside into the lung-searing cold and stepped to the center of Front Street. He counted to three and tossed the hot water into the air, where it vaporized instantly and, just as quickly, transformed into a fine dust of snow that settled around us.

We all wanted to get our own cups of boiling water and make snow, but before we could go inside we sensed something ghostlike and silent passing overhead and looked up. We caught just a glimpse of it, barely above the streetlights—a majestic white owl disappearing into the night.

Season of Snow and Books

Winter is the best season for reading. For me it's a habit that goes back to age eighteen, when my parents and younger brother moved to Kentucky while I stayed in our house on Long Lake. I started college that fall but it didn't work out, so I decided to spend the winter alone, getting educated.

Every morning started the same. There was comfort in it. I dressed, walked down the hill to the lake, cut holes in the ice with an iron spud, and set tip-ups baited with minnows. I returned to the house, built a fire in the fireplace, made breakfast, and started reading. I would read all day, breaking only to tend the fire and go to the picture window in the living room and inspect my tip-ups through binoculars. If a fish grabbed the bait and began unspooling line, the tip-up's red flag sprang upright. Then I would hurry to put on my coat and boots and run down the hill to see what I had caught. I still have the log I kept that winter, with its hand-drawn map keyed to show every fish I caught: a four-pound walleye from a hole straight out from the neighbor's house; two small walleye and a 28-inch pike just over the drop-off; a magnificent seven-pound brown trout in the deep water near the island. There were many others. I taught myself to broil walleye filets in the oven, to fry potatoes until they browned to just the right color and crispness. Sometimes I invited friends to share the bounty, but usually I ate alone at the kitchen table, facing the lake. Even while I ate, I read.

My friend John Klepetka stopped by with two cardboard boxes filled with science-fiction paperbacks, and I read straight through to the bottom of each. Every week or two I drove to the Sixth Street library and searched the stacks, letting serendipity guide me. Picking books from the shelves was like selecting items from a menu in a foreign language. I jabbed blindly, grabbed a book, and opened it to the first page. I couldn't have described what I was looking for, but I recognized it when I found it. Much later I realized I was searching for the voice of the author. If the voice was strong and authentic the book "spoke" to me and I took it home.

I knew there was such a thing as serious literature—not simply a diversion or information on a page, but literature that produced a deeper reading experience and required effort to appreciate. How it worked was still a mystery. I stumbled onto Thomas Wolfe's *Look Homeward, Angel*, and was overcome with sensations. The sentences were more lush and evocative than any I'd ever read. I paused over the phrase "the light came and went and came again" and was suddenly transported to a Southern town on a hot afternoon. I stood in the town square, beside a fountain, with a mist of spray wetting my face whenever the breeze came up. A line of cumulus clouds crossed the sky, and every time a cloud covered the sun a shadow darkened the town square and made the air suddenly cooler. The cloud passed, the sun came out again, and the heat returned.

I was stunned. How could eight words convey so much? Could Wolfe have used more words to achieve the same result? Probably not. That simple phrase, with its few spare words—"the light came and went and came again"—worked because it required my imagination to complete it. Reading was not passive, I realized, it was active. It was an active collaboration between the author and the reader.

Vonnegut, Kerouac, Updike, Roth—I discovered many great authors that year, mostly men, because I was looking for clues for how to be one. I also found writers with Michigan connections, for I was thrilled to think that my home could be a subject worthy of literature. Hemingway's Nick Adams stories electrified me—here was the northern Michigan I knew so well brought vividly to life. Other Michigan writers were new to me, including historian Bruce Catton, novelist and essayist Robert Traver, and poet/novelist Jim Harrison.

For the first time I recognized the enormous differences among authors and the depths to which they could take a reader. I would read a sentence that resonated like a tapped wine glass and feel a physical shudder. That's *true*, I would realize, and know that truth had power in it and that even the ugliest truths were somehow beautiful. I saw too that every sentence and word contained energy. A good book was loaded with that energy, and when you unpacked it, it illuminated everything around you. Experience is complicated—I already knew that, everyone does; you can't last ten minutes on a school playground without learning it—but I had not known how complicated. Books were a record of that complexity. They demonstrated that people everywhere and in all times have felt the same emotions, the same triumphs and defeats, the same pleasures and pains, the same bewilderments and wonders.

The more I read, the more I wanted to read. One evening many years later, when my son Aaron was seventeen, he looked up from his dinner with a stricken expression and said, "Even while I'm *eating* I'm getting hungry." My appetite for books was like that. Now there was no going back. One book led to another, and every author suggested other authors. Without knowing it, I had begun my formal education.

By spring I was not only a reader, but a writer. Suddenly I was filling notebooks because I had no choice. The words flowed as if I had somehow opened a tap to a reservoir I hadn't known existed. And although nothing I wrote would have been of interest to others, I noticed that every now and then, maybe once every five pages, a sentence jumped a few inches into the air and gave off some wattage. Gradually it became clear that those were the sentences that mattered. Much of what was most perplexing and painful in my life, I discovered, could be clarified and made manageable by putting it into words. Filling notebooks that winter with clumsy sentences struggling to be true was my first significant act of adulthood and it set the course for the rest of my life.

All these years later I still think of winter as reading season. On many evenings, while the wind howls outside and snowflakes streak across the windows, I sit in my easy chair near the fireplace, reading books in lamplight, sensing the stunning, beautiful, and heartbreaking complexity of the world—and know that I'm a lucky man.

Acknowledgments

My deepest thanks to the brilliant and gifted Glenn Wolff, without whom my books would be vastly diminished. I'm fortunate to have him as a friend and collaborator.

Somewhat different versions of many of the essays in this book first appeared as "Reflections" columns in *Michigan Blue Magazine*. Many thanks to editors Lisa Jensen and Howard Meyerson for their guidance and encouragement.

Other essays first appeared, often in somewhat different form and under different titles, in the publications below. My thanks to the editors, especially Tom Carney, Jeff Smith, Dave Mull, and Dave Scroppo.

"Water, Water": *Chevy Outdoors*
"The Color of Steelhead": *Midwest Flyfishing, Great Lakes Angler*
"An April Shower": *Canoe and Kayak, Traverse Magazine*
"Island Song": *Sports Afield*
"The Wind on the Beach": *Michigan: Our Land, Our Water, Our Heritage*, edited by John Knott (University of Michigan Press, 2008)
"Ways of Seeing Sleeping Bear": Introduction to *Art of the Sleeping Bear Dunes*, edited by Linda Young (Leelanau Press, 2013)
"Shorewalking": *Traverse Magazine*
"Summer Work and High Water": *Leelanau: A Portrait of Place in Photographs and Text*, by Ken Scott and Jerry Dennis (Petunia Press, 2000)
"The Many Autumns": *Dunes Review, Orion*
"A Fall of Woodcock," "A Double Between the Rivers," and "That Time It Rained": *Upland Almanac*
"Ken Scott's Ice Caves": Introduction to *Ice Caves of Leelanau: A Visual Exploration*, by Ken Scott (Leelanau Press, 2014)
"Star Matter": *Traverse Magazine*